THE CASE AGAINST THE NEW CENSORSHIP

Also by Alan Dershowitz

Cancel Culture: The Latest Attack on Free Speech and Due Process

Confirming Justice—Or Injustice: A Guide to Judging RBG's Successor

The Case for Liberalism in an Age of Extremism: or, Why I Left the Left But Can't Join the Right

Defending the Constitution: Alan Dershowitz's Senate Argument Against Impeachment

Guilt by Accusation: The Challenge of Proving Innocence in the Age of #MeToo

Defending Israel: The Story of My Relationship with My Most Challenging Client

The Mueller Report (with an Introduction by Alan Dershowitz)

The Case Against Impeaching Trump

The Case Against BDS: Why Singling Out Israel for Boycott Is Anti-Semitic and Anti-Peace

Trumped Up: How Criminalization of Political Differences Endangers Democracy

Electile Dysfunction: A Guide for Unaroused Voters

The Case Against the Iran Deal

Terror Tunnels: The Case for Israel's Just War Against Hamas

Abraham: The World's First (But Certainly Not Last) Jewish Lawyer

Taking the Stand: My Life in the Law

The Trials of Zion

The Case for Moral Clarity: Israel, Hamas and Gaza

The Case Against Israel's Enemies: Exposing Jimmy Carter and Others Who Stand in the Way of Peace

Is There a Right to Remain Silent? Coercive Interrogation and the Fifth Amendment After 9/11

Finding Jefferson: A Lost Letter, a Remarkable Discovery and the First Amendment in the Age of Terrorism

Blasphemy: How the Religious Right is Hijacking Our Declaration of Independence

Pre-emption: A Knife That Cuts Both Ways

What Israel Meant to Me: By 80 Prominent Writers, Performers, Scholars, Politicians and Journalists

Rights From Wrongs: A Secular Theory of the Origins of Rights

America on Trial: Inside the Legal Battles That Transformed Our Nation

The Case for Peace: How the Arab-Israeli Conflict Can Be Resolved

The Case for Israel

America Declares Independence

Why Terrorism Works: Understanding the Threat, Responding to the Challenge

Shouting Fire: Civil Liberties in a Turbulent Age

Letters to a Young Lawyer

Supreme Injustice: How the High Court Hijacked Election 2000

Genesis of Justice: Ten Stories of Biblical Injustice that Led to the Ten Commandments and Modern Law

Just Revenge

Sexual McCarthyism: Clinton, Starr, and the Emerging Constitutional Crisis

The Vanishing American Jew: In Search of Jewish Identity for the Next Century

Reasonable Doubts: The Criminal Justice System and the O.J. Simpson Case

The Abuse Excuse: And Other Cop-Outs, Stories and Evasions of Responsibility

The Advocate's Devil

Contrary to Popular Opinion

Chutzpah

Taking Liberties: A Decade of Hard Cases, Bad Laws, and Bum Raps

Reversal of Fortune: Inside the Von Bülow Case

The Best Defense

Criminal Law: Theory and Process (with Joseph Goldstein and Richard Schwartz)

Psychoanalysis, Psychiatry, and Law (with Joseph Goldstein and Jay Katz)

THE CASE AGAINST THE NEW CENSORSHIP

*Protecting Free Speech from Big
Tech, Progressives, and Universities*

ALAN
DERSHOWITZ

HOT BOOKS

Hot Books may be purchased in bulk at special discounts for sales promotion, corporate gifts, fund-raising, or educational purposes. Special editions can also be created to specifications. For details, contact the Special Sales Department, Skyhorse Publishing, 307 West 36th Street, 11th Floor, New York, NY 10018 or info@skyhorsepublishing.com.

Hot Books® and Skyhorse Publishing® are registered trademarks of Skyhorse Publishing, Inc.®, a Delaware corporation.

Visit our website at www.hotbookspress.com.

10 9 8 7 6 5 4 3 2

Library of Congress Cataloging-in-Publication Data is available on file.

ISBN: 978-1-5107-6773-7
eBook: 978-1-5107-6774-4

Cover design by Brian Peterson

Printed in the United States of America

Contents

Introduction: The New Censors: Can Freedom of Speech Be Saved from "Progressives," Social Media, and Universities?   1

Chapter 1: The Events Leading Up to the Free-Speech Crisis: Was the Election Fair?   49

Chapter 2: Impeachment and Censorship for a Speech that Is Constitutionally Protected by the First Amendment   73

Chapter 3: Violent Responses to Speech and Incitement   137

Conclusion: Looking Backward to Show Us the Way Forward   159

Acknowledgements:

Thanks to Maura Kelley for her help in assembling, in organizing, and in typing the manuscript; to Aaron Voloj for his research assistance; to Tony Lyons, Oren Eades, and Brian Peterson for their help in producing the final product; and to my wife Carolyn, my son Elon, my daughter Ella, and her fiance David for their constructive criticisms.

Dedication:

This book is dedicated to my former student, my friend, and my colleague for more than half a century: Harvey Silverglate, an unyielding civil libertarian and an uncompromising defender of free speech.

THE CASE
AGAINST THE NEW
CENSORSHIP

The New Censors: Can Freedom of Speech Be Saved from "Progressives," Social Media, and Universities?

F reedom of speech in America is facing the greatest threats since the Alien and Sedition acts of 1798, which unconstitutionally punished "false, scandalous or malicious writing" against the United States.[1]

Today's threats are even greater than during McCarthyism. This is true for three important reasons:

---

1   Although the U.S. Supreme Court never explicitly ruled that the Alien and Sedition Act was unconstitutional, the Court has implied that it would be held unconstitutional today. In *The New York Times* v. Sullivan, the Court declared, "Although the Sedition Act was never tested in this Court, the attack upon its validity has carried the day in the court of history." 376 U.S. 254, 276 (1964). In a concurring opinion in Watts v. United States, Justice Douglas noted, "The Alien and Sedition Laws constituted one of our sorriest chapters; and I had thought we had done with them forever... Suppression of speech as an effective police measure is an old, old device, outlawed by our Constitution." Watts v. United States, 394 U.S. 705 (1969).

First, today's censorship comes, for the most part, from so-called progressives, who are far more influential and credible than the reactionaries who promoted and implemented McCarthyism. The current efforts to censor politically incorrect and "untruthful" views are led by young people, academics, high tech innovators and writers— yes, writers! These self-righteous and self-appointed Solons of what is and is not permissible speech represent our future, whereas the McCarthyite censors were a throwback to the past— a last gasp of repression from a dying political order.

The new censors are our future leaders. They are quickly gaining influence over the social media, the newsrooms of print and TV, the academy, and other institutions that control the flow of information that impacts all aspects of American political life. These censorial zealots will soon be the CEOs, editors-in-chief, deans, and government officials who run our nation. They are destined to have even more influence over what we can read, see, and hear. If today's attitudes toward freedom of speech by many millennials become tomorrow's rules, our nation will lose much of its freedom of thought, expression, and dissent. Those of us who cherish these freedoms must become more proactive in their defense.

Second, these new progressive censors base their opposition to untrammeled freedom of expression on policies supported by many Americans, especially centrist liberals: anti-racism, anti-sexism, anti-homophobia, anti-hate speech, anti-Holocaust denial, anti-climate denial, and anti-falsehoods. Moreover, these arguments are being offered by people we admire and love. I call them the "good" censors. To paraphrase Pogo: "We have seen the enemy of free speech, and he and she are us!" It is much more difficult to combat *us* than *they*.

Third, the current regime of censorship is more dangerous because for the most part it is not prohibited by the First Amendment: it is promulgated and enforced by private parties who have their own First Amendment rights, rather than by government agents who are bound by the Constitution to "make no law … abridging the freedom of speech." When the government suppresses speech—as it did during McCarthyism by means of Congressional Committee and other state actors—such suppressions can be challenged in the courts, as they were during the 1950s. To be sure, some of the McCarthyite suppression came from private media companies, such as Hollywood studios and television networks (blacklists and "Red Channels").[2] They, too, were more difficult to challenge than governmental censorship and suppression.

During both McCarthyism and the current attack on free speech, the chilling of speech by self-censorship silenced many voices, fearful of recriminations. This, too,

---

2   For a thought-provoking analysis of the Hollywood blacklist, see Victor S. Navasky, *Naming Names* (2003).

is a growing danger that is more difficult to combat than overt governmental censorship.

Nor are these new threats to freedom of speech merely transient reactions to current crises, as McCarthyism proved to be. Today's progressive repression represents changing attitudes among future leaders that may well have enduring consequences beyond the current divisiveness resulting from the Trump presidency.

A) The Trump Factor

Trump himself bears some of the responsibility for stimulating the recent censorial over-reaction. President Trump pushed the First Amendment to its limits—some believe beyond its limits—with his speech before the attack on the Capitol Building, his remarks following the Charlottesville demonstration, and other provocative statements that many regarded as dog whistles. Although some of what he said was reported out of context and without the qualifications he actually added,[3] his words led many—including the

---

3   See Frontline, Trump's American Carnage, Jan. 26, 2021. Much of the media omitted his qualification that his "fine people on both sides" was explicitly inapplicable to neo-Nazis and white nationalists, who he said should be condemned. President Trump said at the press conference after Charlottesville that he was "not talking about the neo-Nazis and the white nationalists—because they should be condemned totally." The media also omitted his call for "peaceful and patriotic" protests at the Capitol. He said at the rally before the riots, "I know that everyone here will soon be marking over to the Capitol building to peacefully and patriotically make your voices heard."

ACLU[4]—to demand limitations on his free speech rights. Once limitations are accepted and imposed on anyone's freedom of expression, a dangerous precedent is established for extending these limitations to unpopular speech by other leaders and ordinary citizens. We are already seeing that happen with efforts to punish members of Congress, lawyers, professors, and ordinary citizens for speeches and statements that were deemed supportive of Trump.

Trump was seen by many on the left, and even some in the center right, as a uniquely dangerous and evil president, whose actions justified extraordinary measures, even measures that compromised constitutional rights and values. The "noble" end of silencing and defeating Trump justified any ignoble means, including denying him and his supporters and enablers the right of free speech, especially on social media.

Some supporters of unconstitutional means seek to justify their censorship and other repressive measures by distorting the Constitution and turning it into a partisan weapon that would have made Jefferson and Madison

---

4   The ACLU supported the second impeachment of President Trump. In a statement, the ACLU wrote that it "believes a president can be impeached for speech that a private citizen could not be prosecuted for," thus implying that Trump's January 6th speech comes within the Brandenburg protection. We can Uphold Free Speech and Hold President Trump Accountable, January 11, 2021, available at https://www.aclu.org/news/civil-liberties/we-can-uphold-free-speech-and-hold-presiden-trump accountable/. (It now says that "Trump's speech was not protected by Brandenburg.")

cringe.[5] Others simply ignore the Constitution and civil liberties in what they honestly believe is a higher calling—namely, to rid us now of Trump and prevent him from running again at any cost, and without regard to long-term dangers to our liberty.

For some liberal opponents of President Trump, this short-term approach posed a conflict with their commitment to civil liberties for everyone, even those whom they despise and fear. Far too few resolved that conflict in favor of our basic liberties. Those of us who did were accused of being Trump enablers, thus deterring many others from incurring that opprobrium. It became dangerous to careers, friendships, and civil discourse to come down on the side of constitutional rights and civil liberties when those rights and liberties happen to support President Trump.[6]

B) The Academic Attacks on Freedom of Speech: Anti-Trump Petitions

Many prominent academics lent their good names to deliberate misinterpretations of the Constitution that they never would have accepted had the shoe been on the other

---

5   See, e.g., Jonathan Turley, Impeachment in the Age of Trump: Laurence Tribe's Evolving Views of Impeachable Conduct, Jan. 29, 2021, available at available at https://jonathanturley.org/2021/01/29/tribe-in-the-age-of-trump-the-evolving-views-of-impeachable-conduct/.

6   Evan Mandery, What Happened to Alan Dershowitz, Politico, May 11, 2018.

foot—had the President been a liberal Democrat whom they supported, rather than President Trump, whose policies and actions they despised. Their partisan hypocrisy was evident to those of us who knew their history,[7] but not as obvious to those who only saw their institutional affiliations and academic pedigrees. They signed petitions that used their scholarly credentials as a cover for their partisan preferences.

One of the most dangerous of the many petitions circulated by those supporting Trump's removal was signed by many prominent constitutional scholars. On the eve of former President Trump's second impeachment trial in the senate, a group of 144 constitutional scholars issued a threatening public letter to his lawyers demanding, in effect, that they not make arguments to the Senate regarding the First Amendment. This demand came in the form of a claim that "any First Amendment defense raised by President Trump's attorneys would be legally frivolous."

This demand is both dangerous to our adversarial system of justice and wrong as a matter of constitutional law. It is dangerous because the rules of professional responsibility prohibit a lawyer from making frivolous arguments, and carry disciplinary sanctions for anyone who does. The letter purported to put Trump's lawyers on notice that if

---

7   See, e.g. Jonathan Turley, Impeachment in the Age of Trump: Laurence Tribe's Evolving Views of Impeachable Conduct, Jan. 29, 2021.

they made any First Amendment arguments, they would be subjecting themselves to possible discipline.

The argument is wrong on its merits as a matter of Constitutional law. But the most dangerous aspect of the letter is that its goal was to chill President Trump's lawyers from making important arguments on behalf of their client. The letter could easily have said that any First Amendment argument would be wrong, but the letter went further and suggested that any such argument is prohibited by the Code of Professional Responsibility, and may result in disciplinary sanctions against any lawyer who makes a frivolous argument.

As a teacher of legal ethics for more than a quarter of a century at Harvard Law School, I know that these 144 experts are wrong. Arguments to the Senate based on the First Amendment are not frivolous. They should be and were offered vigorously and responsibly without fear of ethical consequences. What is of questionable ethics is for the scholars to try to frighten lawyers away from making plausible arguments by threatening that they might face disciplinary consequences for doing so. I offered to support any lawyer who made responsible First Amendment arguments to the Senate and is disciplined as a consequence.

As a constitutional lawyer who has litigated some of the most important First Amendment cases in the last half century—including the Pentagon Papers, I Am

Curious (Yellow), Hair, the Chicago Seven, Frank Snepp, Harry Reams, and Wikileaks – I am relatively confident that the current Supreme Court would find President Trump's ill-advised and justly condemnable speech to be fully protected under the *Brandenburg* principle, which distinguishes between advocacy and incitement to violence. President Trump's words were provocative, but they included a plea for his listeners to protest "peacefully and patriotically." Compared to the speech made by Clarence Brandenburg—a neo-Nazi Klansman surrounded by armed men with crosses—President Trump's speech was pabulum. It was typical of rousing speeches made by radicals, union leaders, suffragettes, and some Democratic politicians in our nation's capital and elsewhere. It was far less incendiary than the speeches made by anti-war activists during the Democratic national convention of 1968 (the Chicago Seven).

Not only would this Supreme Court conclude that the speech was protected advocacy, so would prior Supreme Courts during the golden age of the First Amendment, which extended from the early 1960s to the beginning of the 21st century. Justices Holmes, Brandeis, and Jackson would also have found this speech to be well within the protections of the First Amendment. The letter itself conceded that only *some* of the signers—not all—agree with its conclusion about the speech being outside the protections of *Brandenburg*. How then could it be frivolous for Trump's lawyers to offer such an argument?

The argument that the First Amendment "simply does not apply" to impeachment cases flies in the face of the text, which prohibits "Congress" from making any law abridging "the freedom of speech." The courts have interpreted this to include any state action, whether in the form of a formal law or any other consequential act. Once again, it would be one thing if the letter had merely said that this argument is wrong, but to say it is frivolous is dangerous and irresponsible.

The letter also states that "no reasonable scholar or jurist" would make these First Amendment arguments. This sends a chilling message to current and prospective law teachers: if you want to be considered a "reasonable scholar or jurist" by your peers and hiring committees, don't you dare make these constitutional arguments in the court of public opinion. Well, I, for one, continued to make them, and I challenged the signatories to the letter to debate me about whether my arguments are reasonable or frivolous. None accepted.

First Amendment issues should have been and were vigorously presented to the Senate without fear of being branded frivolous and thus unethical or unreasonable and thus disqualifying as a scholar or jurist. To try to intimidate lawyers from making them by declaring them frivolous and irresponsible is a form of prior censorship, inconsistent with the spirit of our constitutional system.

Another outrageous petition was by hundreds of authors, journalists, editors, publishers, agents, and others in the media demanding that no one who "participated in the administration of Donald Trump" should have their "philosophies" published and given "the imprimatur of respectability." They say that they "believe in the power of words" and that is why they seek to deny that power to "the monsters among us, and will do whatever is in our power to stop" enriching these "monsters"—a word that speaks volumes about the growing intolerance toward differing political views – by publishing their books and other writings. [8]

Similar petitions are being circulated by students, faculty, lawyers and others who claim the mantle of being progressives and do-gooders. These include petitions at several universities demanding that anyone who participated in, enabled or supported the Trump Administration be censored as a speaker, be cancelled as a potential teacher, and be required to acknowledge their wrongdoing and subject themselves to some sort of moral reprogramming.[9] The

---

8   See Alison Flood, Open Letter Calls for Publishing Boycott of Trump Administration Memoirs, The Guardian, Jan. 19, 2021, available at https://www.theguardian.com/books/2021/jan/19/open-letter-calls-for-publishing-boycott-of-trump-administration-memoirs

9   Harvard students published an open letter calling for a new "system of accountability" to review top political appointees who served under

Harvard Law School petition demands that "people who condone and participate in anti-democratic, racist, xenophobic, and immoral practices have no home at Harvard," and should not be allowed "back into polite society." A ban on such people would "teach ambitious students of all ages that attempting to subvert the democratic process" will be bad for their "success and prestige." Thousands of lawyers, professors, and law students have petitioned to disbar and/or discipline lawyers who "denigrated democratic institutions," "betray the very democratic institutions they are charged with protecting," or show "no respect for the constitution."[10]

C) Comparisons to McCarthyism

These are precisely the kinds of vague, anti-patriotic accusations that were levelled against lawyers who represented alleged Communists and "fellow travelers," and that led to the call for "loyalty" tests and oaths by Senator McCarthy and his minions. Bar associations and character

---

Republican President Donald Trump and could come to campus as professors, fellows or speakers after Trump leaves office. The petition claimed that those who failed to uphold traditional democratic principles should be disqualified. "A complete disregard for the truth is a defining feature of many decisions made by this administration. That alone should be enough to draw a line." Collin Binkley, Harvard Petition Demands Scrutiny of Ex-Trump Officials, AP News, Nov. 20, 2020

10   See e.g., Thousands of Lawyers, Law Students Push to Disbar Cruz, Hawley, Bloomberg, Jan. 11, 2021.

committees disqualified, as unpatriotic, lawyers who failed
to pass such tests because of their radical left-wing views
or associations.[11] True civil libertarians—even those who
despise Communism—opposed such McCarthyite repri-
sals, arguing that American lawyers, and ordinary citizens,
must remain free to criticize *all* aspects of our system of governance, including the Constitution and democratic institutions, as many radicals have done throughout history.[12]

The new progressive censors must understand this history if it is not to be turned against them in the future.
Precedents established today against the right will lie
about like loaded weapons to be deployed against the left
tomorrow. Indeed, repression in the United States has been
directed at the left more often than against the right. Past
may become prologue when it comes to repression.

In the late 1940s and early 1950s, it was the fear of
Communism that fueled the censorship of the McCarthyite
right. Over the past four years, it was the fear of Trumpism
—and of President Trump himself—that escalated and
energized a nascent left-wing movement toward censorship

---

11   James Moliterno, Politically Motivated Bar Discipline, Washington
University Law Review, 725, 729 (2005).
      The Harvard Law Review, which accepted editors based on their grades,
disqualified a student who had been accused of Communist affiliations.

12   In their brief advocating the second impeachment of Donald Trump,
the House managers argue that the First Amendment does not protect
attacks on democracy.

and cancelation of many on the right and even in the center. Too few civil libertarians have risen to the challenge of defending the rights of Americans accused of supporting Trump. In some civil liberties circles, it is more acceptable to defend the rights of Neo-Nazis to march through Jewish neighborhoods and hold anti-Semitic signs than it is to defend Donald Trump's freedom of speech.

I came of age during the era of McCarthyism, but I never understood until now how decent people—friends and relatives I admired – could support suppression of free speech and due process and other denials of basic liberties. Some of my professors at Brooklyn College supported McCarthyism. These included such distinguished scholars as Professor Eugene Scalia, father of Justice Scalia, as well as several professors who had emigrated to America from Hungry, Czechoslovakia, and other countries under the thrall of Communism. In all other respects, these were decent, sensitive, and liberty-loving people who had one significant flaw: their support for repressive McCarthyism. Their experience with Communist oppression gave them a blind spot with regard to the rights of those suspected of Communist affiliation. I simply could not understand it, because I viewed McCarthyism as totally and unequivocally evil—just as I viewed Communism. I could not understand how good people could support such a bad policy. I hated Communism, but I didn't personally fear it. It never occurred to me that Communists could ever get a foothold in the United States. I personally knew no Communists, except for the occasional oddball who would hand out leaflets in the neighborhood. To me Communism was a hollow threat—a straw man—that was being used as an excuse for repression. I simply could not identify with anyone who would suppress the rights of individuals accused of Communism or communist affiliation.

Now that I see good and decent people demanding censorship and denial of due process for those who collaborated with Trump, I have a better understanding of what I grew up with. These modern day McCarthyites of the left were genuinely afraid of Donald Trump and what he stood for. They really believed, as did some of the McCarthyites I knew during the 1950s, that giving free speech rights to those who they feared would bring about catastrophe. For them, both then and now, the noble end of preventing the victory of Communism or Trumpism justified any means, including even the most ignoble and repressive.

I recall being asked by some supporters of McCarthyism at Brooklyn College how I could defend the rights of Communists, who, if they came to power, would deny me my rights of free speech. I was asked similar questions by friends who saw my support for President Trump's constitutional rights as enabling a president who would deny those basic rights to others. The similarities are striking and frightening. The essence of democracy is assuring rights *even* to those who would deny them to you. The Constitution is not a suicide pact, but nor is it a license to deny liberty in response to any perceived threat to safety.

As Benjamin Franklin cautioned: "Those who would give up essential liberty to purchase a little temporary safety, deserve neither liberty nor safety." We must sometimes compromise safety in the short-term to protect liberty in the long term. In extreme situations, we may even have to compromise some liberties in order to protect ourselves.[13] But freedom of speech—freedom to criticize governments and other institutions—should never be among them.

Jefferson was being somewhat Pollyannaish when he assured us that "we have nothing to fear from the demoralizing reasonings of some, if others are left free to demonstrate their errors,"[14] but he was surely correct when he warned us that we have much to fear from the "varying consciences" of the censors.

D) Jefferson's Free Speech Arguments

Several years ago, I engaged in a mock "dialogue" with Jefferson about his claim that we have "nothing to fear"

---

13   E.g., Ex parte Milligan, 71 U.S. (4 Wall.) 2 (1866) and Ex parte Merryman, 17 F. Cas. 144 (1861).

14   For a discussion of this quotation, see Alan Dershowitz, *Finding, Framing and Hanging Jefferson*, Ch. 8 (2009).

from freedom of speech. I argued that freedom of speech is not as cost free as he believed. Sometimes the open marketplace of ideas produces bad, even dangerous, falsehoods and actions. The implicit premise of the "marketplace" analogy is that if the marketplace of ideas remains open to all, then the "good" ideas will drive out the "bad" ones. This is an entirely empirical and experiential claim, and it is—I respectfully believe—not always true. The argument presupposes that if all ideas are allowed to be expressed, the marketplace will see to it that good ideas drive out the bad. A variant on Adam Smith's invisible hand—or what Jefferson believed was a universal "moral sense"—is presumed to be at work. The problem is that the metaphor to economic markets simply is inapt, and the existence of some inherent moral sense, in which Jefferson and many of his colleagues believed, is questionable.[15] (I think the comedian Rita Rudner came closer to the truth when she said that "human nature is largely something that has to be overcome.")

History has repeatedly proved that bad ideas sometimes drive out good ones and that the marketplace of ideas is at best highly inefficient. Winston Churchill observed, based on his experiences, that "A lie gets halfway around the world before the truth has a chance to get its pants on." This observation is even truer today than when it was made years ago because technology is quicker, and

---

15   Mark Hauser, Moral Minds: The Nature of Right and Wrong (2007).

fascinating lies are often more interesting to the media than boring truths. Twitter and other platforms host thousands of lies, defamations, and crackpot rants every hour, and the truthful responses are drowned out by the flood of falsehoods. Jefferson seemed to acknowledge that the marketplace can produce false beliefs when he observed later in his life that "the man who never looks into a newspaper is better informed than he who reads them."[16] Today, people who don't watch certain TV channels and don't read certain websites are "better informed" than those who do. The truth is a powerful weapon, but so is the lie. And the honest truth does not always win out over the clever lie.

Even if the marketplace were an apt analogy, in most markets the golden rule prevails: he who has the gold rules. Speech is not free in a market-driven economy; it can be quite expensive. Thus, the new censors argue, quite persuasively, that freedom of speech can be a weapon to be bought by the rich against the poor or by the privileged against the underprivileged. This observation, while largely true, is not a good argument for censorship, which can also be weaponized by the powerful against the powerless. Making speech more accessible to all—as the internet does, at least to some degree – is a far better response to the golden rule. But it, too, comes with heavy costs.

---

16   Thomas Jefferson, Letter to John Norvell, June 11, 1807.

E) The Costs of Liberty

Jefferson's argument is part of a generally flawed approach to civil liberties that prevails, even today, among some absolutists. The absolutist refuses to recognize that we must often make choices among evils. Consider, for example, the debate about torture that has been roiling the civilized world since 9/11. Many civil libertarians refuse to recognize that there is even a conflict between liberty and security. They assume—assert, pretend—that torture *never* works because a person under torture will *always* provide *false* information. If only that were true, it would immediately end any rational debate about the use of torture under any circumstances.

The reality, however, is more complicated. Torture often fails to produce true and useful information, for the reasons correctly offered by civil libertarians. But it sometimes does produce such information, as evidenced by the fact that members of the French resistance during World War II were caught and executed after their brave colleagues were tortured into revealing their whereabouts.[17] No reasonable interrogator would ever *believe* any statement produced under torture, but that is not how torture words in barbaric societies (or even in less barbaric ones). The torturer does

---

17   Alan Dershowitz, Why Terrorism Works, Ch. 4, Yale University Press (2003). Alan Dershowitz, Tortured Reasoning, Ch. 14, in Sanford Levinson, Torture: A Collection (Oxford University Press, 2006).

not seek *statements* from his victim (unless he is trying to secure a confession, and he doesn't care whether it's true or false). He seeks self-proving preventive information. "Take me to where the bombs are hidden." "Show me the plans." "Call your collaborator and tell him to meet you some-where."[18] We should, in my view, seek to abolish torture, not because it never works, but rather because even if it does sometimes work, the moral calculus applied by dem-ocratic societies should reject the use of torture, despite its occasionally useful results. That is the honest argument civil libertarians and politicians refuse to make. The rea-son they refuse to make it is that if they were candid, they would have to concede that they are willing to see some innocent people killed by terrorist, rather than to permit terrorists to be tortured.

Civil liberty absolutists, in my experience, are often reluctant to acknowledge that they are making difficult trade-offs—choices of evils, or tragic choices. There are few "free lunches" when it comes to civil liberties.

Virtually all complex issues require a choice of evils. Freedom of speech is certainly among them. We do have something to fear from the expression of dangerous opin-ions, even if they are countered in the marketplace of ideas. First, there are often no marketplaces, only monopolies.

---

18   Ibid.

That is certainly becoming the case with social media. We have much to fear in such situations, as evidenced by the effect of Nazi propaganda on Germans and others throughout Europe, as evidenced by the impact of the incitements to tribal genocide in the African nation of Rwanda, and as evidenced by the effect that the speeches of imams have had on suicide bombers who are being used today against the United States and other nations. Rabbi Meir Kahane, the late head of the Jewish Defense League, certainly had blood on his hands for some of the speeches he made and the way he inspired young, naïve JDL members to plant bombs. And he operated in an open marketplace of ideas. I know, because I was part of that marketplace, urging his young Jewish followers to eschew violence.

It is certainly possible that President Trump's exercise of his freedom of speech may have had an impact, even if unintended, on some who subsequently engaged in violence. It is also possible that some left-wing agitators may have inspired violence among some of their followers. That is a price we pay for freedom of speech, and we should acknowledge its cost and argue that it is worth it.

F) The Costs of Censorship

Freedom of speech should be protected not because the marketplace of ideas *assures* that the good will drive out the bad, but despite the reality that the bad will *sometimes* prevail. The same is true of free elections, which are the truest market-place of political choice. Hitler received the most votes in the German free election of 1932, and other terrible candidates have beaten far better candidates in free elections. But ending free elections is not the answer to bad results. Free speech should also be permitted despite its occasional bad results, because the alternative is more dangerous. Any system of censorship must either be pervasive or selective. There can never be just "a little" censorship. The choice is between what I call "the taxicab theory of free speech" and a "system of censorship." Just as a taxi cab must accept all law-abiding passengers who can pay the fare, without discriminating on the basis of where they were going or why they are going there, so, too, a government or a university should not pick and choose between what speeches, books, or magazines may be offensive. Once it gets into the business of picking and choosing among viewpoints, then it must create a fair and equitable *system* of censorship based on articulated principles. If it decides that items offensive to some women can be banned, then it will have difficulty rejecting the claims of offensiveness made by African-Americans, Jews, homosexuals, fundamentalist Christians, atheists, vegetarians, anti-fur proponents, and other politically correct and incorrect groups. I call this "-ism equity." Both alternatives—pervasive censorship and -ism equity—produce less freedom of expression.

G) Social Media Censorship

The social media are facing precisely this dilemma now. In addition to demands for equal treatment, any institution that edits selectively on the basis of the alleged *falsity* of the censored material faces the following conundrum: if Facebook, Twitter, and YouTube take down content which they deem to be *untrue*, then at least some viewers may come to believe that content that is *not* taken down must have passed the test of *truthfulness*. That is surely misleading at best, since the vast majority of untrue content is *not* taken down. So, when social media get into the business of selectively censoring some untruths, it is *they* who may be promoting false belief in the alleged truth of the untruths they do not censor. It is a no-win situation.

An analogy from governmental regulation of speech may be instructive. There are but two pure models of the role of the state in relation to offensive speech. Under the first – whose paradigm was the former Soviet Union—the state must literally approve everything that is officially published (hence the term *samizdat*—illegally self-published without approval of the state). Everything that is published thus reflects affirmative government policy. Everything turned down for publication is against governmental policy. There are no neutral publications that are neither approved nor disapproved by the state but merely tolerated. There are no gray zones. No Soviet high official was ever heard to say to an author, "I disagree with what you are saying, but I will defend your right to say it."

The second pure model is one that no nation in history has ever achieved. But ours comes closest to it, at least at times. The model is one of complete content neutrality. The state neither approves nor disapproves of what is published in the newspapers, magazines, TV, or the internet. Indeed, it does not even learn what is being published until after it has hit the streets or the internet (hence the importance of the prohibition against *prior* restraint). When an offensive item is published, the government can—and should—disclaim all responsibility for its content. The content, simply put, is none of the government's business: the government has neither approved it nor disapproved it.

Once the government gets into the business of disapproving of content on grounds of offensiveness, it has lost its claim to neutrality, and the trouble begins.

Assume that a group of militant feminists argues to a local government that a particular pornographic film—say, *Deep Throat*—is so offensive to women that it should be banned. Officials view the film, agree with the feminists, and ban it from their city. The next week, a group of blacks argues that the film *Birth of a Nation* is at least as offensive to blacks as *Deep Throat* is to women; a group of Jews will argue that the Nazi films of Leni Riefenstahl are at least as offensive as *Birth of a Nation* and *Deep Throat*; a group of gays will make the same claim about the film *Cruising*.

If there is one thing that is clear about offensiveness, it is that there is no objective basis for comparison. If obscenity is in the eye of the beholder—or, as Justice William O. Douglas once quipped, "in the crotch of the beholder"— then offensiveness lies deep in the history and psyche of those who feel it. Can anyone—especially a government— make any comparative assessment of the offensiveness felt by a concentration camp survivor seeing a swastika, a descendant of a slave seeing a burning cross, a woman who has been raped seeing the horrible portrayal of sexual brutalization? If the government is to ban one, it must ban all. If it is to *refuse* to ban any, it must refuse to ban all.

Let me tell you a story from my own experience. I once represented Soviet dissidents at a Helsinki Human Rights conference. During a meeting with Soviet officials, I complained about the recent publication of certain blatantly anti-Semitic material. The official responded—quite expectedly—by telling me that worse material was published in the United States. I agreed and took out copies of some horrible anti-Semitic material published here and showed them to him. I also showed him some of the copies of the material published in the Soviet Union. I asked him to look at both and tell me the difference. He understood immediately: The Soviet material bore a stamp signifying that it had been approved by Glavlit, the official censor-ship agency of the Soviet Union. The American material had been approved by no one except the National Socialist White People's party—whose stamp it bore. The Soviet material was awful; the American material was worse. But the Soviet material carried the imprimatur of its govern-ment—a government that will not allow the publication of material deemed offensive by *favored* groups but will encourage the publication of material deemed offensive to *disfavored* groups. Therein lies the difference—and a criti-cal difference it is.

What does all this have to do with social media? Social media is not government, but it, too, must have a policy in relation to offensive material. And although there are considerable differences between government and social media, the latter can learn a great deal from the mistakes of governments.

The major social media began with a model of neutral-ity, but have now largely abandoned, or at least compro-mised, that model. They have censored content on grounds of offensiveness or untruthfulness. They cannot now claim that they never succumb to pressure from offended groups. The best they can do is point to certain instances where they have resisted pressures. But they must then acknowl-edge that they have also succumbed and compromised on other occasions.

The social media can point out that they are less monolithic than governments, that their content is neither approved nor disapproved by a single centralized authority. Approval and disapproval decisions are made by groups of individual and algorithms coded by individuals.

But nor can it be said, in fairness, that the social media have come close to the Soviet model of total approval or disapproval. There are gray areas where potential censors have said, "We disagree with your decision, but we will defend your right to stand by it."

The social media will continue to live in a twilight zone—a gray area—of censorship. Is it possible to live within that gray area and still maintain a considerable amount of freedom and integrity? I believe the answer is a qualified yes—if the right steps are taken *in advance*.

The two starting points —really poles—in any intelligent discussion of censorship based on offensiveness or untruth are, one, the *government* should *not* engage in content censorship based on offensiveness or untruth; and, two, private individuals and groups are absolutely entitled to express objections to speech that they find offensive or false. Indeed, the open marketplace of ideas presupposes vigorous response—and objection—to offensive or false speech. As William Safire once juxtaposed these two points, "Every American has the right to complain about the trash on TV—except Uncle Sam."

H) Economic Censorship

But these two poles do not provide answers to the really hard questions, such as: To what extent is it appropriate— put aside legal – for a group that feels strongly about certain speech to express their objections through concerted economic pressures? Economic pressures surely cannot be ignored in any discussion of free speech. For if, to paraphrase George Bernard Shaw, assassination is the ultimate form of censorship, then bankruptcy is surely a penultimate form of censorship in a profit-motivated society. The website *Gawker* was put out of business by a lawsuit financed by a wealthy critic.[19]

Most people answer the economic question differently, depending on which side of the dispute they happen to fall on. I know many feminists who were adamantly opposed to the McCarthyite Hollywood blacklist, but who strongly favor boycotting general bookstores that include allegedly sexist material (such as *Penthouse, Playboy,* and *Hustler*) among their fare. Are there really any principled distinctions? Would they justify, as an exercise of free speech, an organized boycott by "pro-lifers" against a small-town bookstore that

---

19   See, e.g., Peter Thiel Makes Offer to Buy Gawker, the News Site He Helped Bankrupt, *The Guardian,* Jan. 11, 2018.

sold books advocating abortion or birth control? Would the African American or Jew who boycotts a general bookstore selling Nazi and Klan material justify the boycott of a store selling evolutionary or anti-gun-control tracts? What would be left for the bookstore to sell if every group that objected to particular books boycotted the store? We used to be able to say that the store would be selling only books like *Mary Poppins* or *Harry Potter*, but even those books have recently been subject to censorial efforts.

Is it possible to articulate general rules—rules of civility, rules of morality, rules of law, rules of constitutionality—that do not depend on whose ox is being gored or which group is being insulted? I have never seen it done.

What about organized boycotts of advertisers who sponsor content deemed deeply offensive to certain groups? Can we devise neutral rules for when such boycotts for legitimate and when they're illegitimate? Again, we can begin at the extremes. Surely it is more appropriate to boycott an advertiser who plays an active role in determining content than one who plays no role. If, for example, a sponsor was to say, "I'll advertise on this platform only if it puts down gays, or Blacks, or Jews," then the propriety of an economic boycott becomes more obvious. But if the sponsor merely declines to remove his ad from objectionable content, the propriety of a general product boycott becomes more questionable. A boycott against a sponsor because of the nature of that sponsor's own advertisements is easier to justify than a boycott of a sponsor because of the content of what is sponsored. A boycott of a specific video is more justifiable than a boycott of an entire platform.[20]

We must persuade the American public that although most boycotts are constitutionally protected, some of them are morally *wrong*. There is, of course, no inconsistency between an expression of speech being *both* constitutionally protected and morally wrong. Hooting down a speaker, hurling racial epithets, and marching through Skokie with Nazi symbols are all examples of constitutionally protected but morally wrong speech. More recently, President Trump's speech that encouraged listeners to march on the Capital "peacefully and patriotically" was constitutionally protected, but reasonable people may conclude that it was morally wrong.

It is morally wrong to exercise your freedom of speech—and freedom of purchase—to restrict the freedom of others to speak and learn what they choose. It is morally wrong—and inconsistent with the premises underlying the First Amendment—to try to shut down a stall in the marketplace of ideas because that stall is selling ideas that are objectionable to you. Set up your own stall and sell better

20 See, Yahoo News, Feb. 2, 2021, My Pillow Guy, Mike Lindell gest cancelled in Newsmax interview: "Retailers like Bed Bath and Beyond have stopped selling my pillow."

ideas. That is what some new social media are doing by creating platforms that do not censor political speech based on content. I applaud that.

I) Dangerous Speech

A more powerful case for freedom of speech than the one offered by Jefferson must acknowledge that speech can be dangerous, that it can cause harmful acts, that the marketplace of ideas is not guarantee of safety. There are no guarantees, except that the costs of imposing a regime of censorship outweigh the costs of tolerating dangerous speech and its consequences. Jefferson's "marketplace of ideas" argument would have been strengthened if he had said that we have *less* to fear from the expression of ideas than we do from their suppression, rather than categorically stating that we have *nothing* to fear, so long as "others are left free to demonstrate their errors."

Freedom of speech, especially on unregulated social media, can be dangerous and harmful, in part because many people believe Jefferson's wrong-headed assumption that the marketplace of ideas is a guarantee of safety

In an ideal world of rational thinkers, Jefferson may well be right. He lived in a world closer to that ideal than we do today. I'm afraid the world we live in today—a world dominated by shouting talk show hosts, nonsensical tweets, conspiratorial websites, cynical image makers, crass opportunists, political pollsters, and leaders who govern by following the polls – is a far cry from the New England town meetings, the Virginia salons, or the Greek amphitheaters where democracy took root. And even in Athens, the ideas expressed by Socrates were greeted not by immediate acceptance but by hemlock. The marketplace of ideas— limited as it may have been in ancient Greece—did not protect Socrates, although his good ideas, or at least those that survived, have been accepted by the marketplace of history. Consider, however, how many good ideas died along with their authors—in the Crusades, the Inquisition, the slave trade, as well as in genocides that have occurred since Jefferson wrote, including the Holocaust, the Stalinist purges in the Soviet Union, genocides in Africa, Cambodia, and Armenia, the Chinese "cultural revolution", and other mass slaughters.

Several years ago, during a speech to hundreds of lawyers in Hamburg, I asked the audience how many of them were victims of the Holocaust. A dozen hands were raised. I then asked how many had lost friends or relatives to cancer, heart attacks, and other illnesses. Every hand went up. I then asked rhetorically, "How can you be sure that the cures for those illnesses did not go up in the smoke of Auschwitz?"

The ideas that survived the skewed marketplace may well constitute but a fraction of those devised by the minds of creative men and women over time. The marketplace of ideas is the best option for a democracy not because it always produces the best ideas, but because like democracy itself, the alternatives are far worse. What Winston Churchill famously said of democracy—"the worst form of government, except for all those other forms that have been tried"—might also be said about the marketplace of ideas. The parallel should not be surprising, since without freedom of speech, democracy cannot survive.

J) Mill's Argument for Free Speech

The great 19th century libertarian philosopher John Stuart Mill also made the case for the open marketplace of ideas, while at the same time rejecting Jefferson's naïve view that we have nothing to fear from freedom of speech.

In his ringing defense of free speech, Mill disputes Jefferson's argument that "the marketplace of ideas" will inevitably produce truth:

"The dictum that truth always triumphs over persecution, is one of those pleasant falsehoods which men repeat after one another till they pass into commonplaces, but which all experience refutes. History teems with instances of truth put down by persecution."[21]

---

21   J.S. Mill, *On Liberty* (1859). In 1993, Bantam Press had asked me to write an introduction to John Stuart Mill's *On Liberty* and *Utilitarianism*, from which this discussion is adapted.

Mill offers this observation in refutation of the empirical claim that "truth may justifiably be persecuted because persecution cannot possibly do it any harm." Persecution can, in fact, destroy truths, not only in the short run, but forever, as we have seen with the earlier examples I have cited. Truth is not a piece of matter or a unit of energy that will survive pummeling and emerge unscathed in one form or another at one time or another. It is a fragile and ethereal aspiration, easily buried, difficult to retrieve, and capable of being lost forever. That is why every time an idea is censored, a person with an idea killed, or a culture destroyed, we risk permanent injury to the corpus of human knowledge. And that is why it is always better to err on the side of more speech, more expression, more advocacy—even when the benefits seem distant and the costs immediate. American jurisprudence and Mill's philosophy reach the same conclusion about the benefits of unfettered exchange, though by somewhat different routes.

Mill argued persuasively even for the freedom to err—the right to be wrong. He offered a utilitarian justification for encouraging false arguments against the received wisdom, because "teachers and learners go to sleep at their post, as soon as there is no enemy in the field."

One of Mill's most compelling arguments has particular applications to the debate over social media censorship, speech codes, identity politics, and political correctness

– especially on contemporary college and university campuses. Mill understood more than a century ago what many proponents of speech codes seem to ignore today: namely, that censorship is almost never content-neutral. Codes that purport to ban "offensive" or "untruthful" words are inevitably invoked selectively against politically incorrect words. Censorship is a weapon wielded by those in power against those who are not. On college and university campuses, those in power—or those who can influence those in power—may be very different from those in power in the outside world, but Mill's point remains persuasive:

"With regard to what is commonly meant by intemperate discussion, namely invective, sarcasm, personality, and the like the denunciation of these weapons would deserve more sympathy if it were ever proposed to interdict them equally to both sides; but it is only desired to restrain the employment of them against the prevailing opinion: against the un-prevailing they may not only be used without general disapproval, but will be likely to obtain for him who uses them the praise of honest zeal and righteous indignation."

Mill would argue, of course, that even if we could create what I have called "a symmetrical circle of civility" or "-ism equity"—namely, the identical rules of discourse for all, regardless of the content of their views—it would still be wrong to restrict speech based on factors such as offensiveness, incivility, rudeness, or falsity.

The hard question for Mill—indeed, for any utilitarian advocate of free speech – is what should happen when freedom of speech clashes with Mill's other important principle: The authorization of state compulsion "to prevent harm to others." Here Mill is not at his best as a thinker:

"No one pretends that actions should be as free as opinions. On the contrary, even opinions lose their immunity, when the circumstances in which they are expressed are such as to constitute their expression a positive instigation to some mischievous act. An opinion that corn-dealers are starvers of the poor or that private property is robbery, ought to be unmolested when simply circulated through the press, but may justly incur punishment when delivered orally to an excited mob assembled before the house of a corn-dealer, or when handed about among the same mob in the form of a placard. Acts, of whatever kind, which, without justifiable cause, do harm to others, may be, and in the more important cases absolutely required to be, controlled by the unfavorable sentiments, and, when needful, by the active interference of mankind. The liberty of the individual must be thus far limited; he must not make himself a nuisance to other people."

Mill's last sentence—that a speaker may not "make himself a nuisance to other people"—contains the seeds of a system of pervasive censorship. Mill probably intended the concept *nuisance* to be construed in the narrowest possible way, say, by reference to his prior example of inciting an excited mob. But it is surely capable of being applied to almost any manner of offensive speech, ranging from religious proselytization, to hate speech, to pornography, to the dog whistles of a controversial president.

Mill's narrow, utilitarian argument for some censorship is, in my view, shortsighted. A larger view would prefer—as the First Amendment to the United States Constitution prefers and as Mill himself seems to prefer elsewhere—the benefits of relatively unabridged speech over the "inconvenience" of tolerating nuisances, even deeply offensive nuisances. One need not agree with the ditty we all learned on the streets— "Sticks and stone may break my bones, but names will never harm me"—to accept the important distinction between the state regulation of "sticks and stones," on the one hand, and of "names" on the other forms of speech, on the other. Justice Louis Brandies provided wiser counsel than Mill when he argued, in a case involving socialists who trespassed on private property as part of a protest against capitalism, that a free and open society should tolerate a certain degree of nuisance as a price worth paying for free and untrammeled expression.[22] We should have different rules for regulating

---

22 "But it is hardly conceivable that this Court would hold constitutional a statute which punished as a felony the mere voluntary assembly with a society formed to teach that pedestrians had the moral right to cross

nonexpressive actions that pose dangers to others and for censoring expressive speech that poses comparable dangers. A single utilitarian calculus simply will not do in a society that values freedom of expression more highly than freedom of action. Our society is committed to the proposition that freedom of expression is the best guarantor of freedom of action. Our First Amendment expresses a far different calculus for regulating speech than for regulating non-expressive conduct, and that is as it should be. Your right to swing your fist should end at the tip of my nose, but your right to express your ideas should not necessarily end at the lobes of my ears.

The marketplace of ideas is a raucous bazaar, in which a bit of discomfort or nuisance is a small price to pay for the benefits of preserving freedom of expression from the voracious and not easily satisfied appetite of the censor.

K) Benevolent Censorship by the Good Guys

An example of what can happen when the marketplace of ideas is replaced by the stamp of the censor occurred during McCarthyism. But back then brave civil libertarians

---

unenclosed, unposted, wastelands and to advocate their doing so, even if there was imminent danger that advocacy would lead to a trespass. The fact that speech is likely to result in some violence or in destruction of property is not enough to justify its suppression. There must be the probability of serious injury to the State. Among free men, the deterrents ordinarily to be applied to prevent crime are education and punishment for violations of the law, not abridgment of the rights of free speech and assembly." Whitney v. California, 274 U.S. 357 (1927) (Brandeis, J., concurring).

stood up against the obvious danger to liberty represented by Senator Joseph McCarthy. Back then, the issue was widely seen as one of evil versus good. McCarthyism was evil. McCarthy himself was evil. Those standing against him—like the great lawyer Joseph Welch, who rhetorically asked him: "At long last, have you left no sense of decency?" – were the good guys. That is not the case with the current attack on free speech that is being *supported* by many who claim the mantle of civil liberties, including the American Civil liberties Union.[23] Because today's attack on free speech is being urged by progressives—by our friends, children, colleagues and others we respect and admire—many civil libertarians are conflicted and remain silent, or prioritize politics over principles, the liberal agenda over civil liberties.

Some of these new censors act as if they have just invented the wheel. They shout eureka as they proclaim that they have just made a remarkable discovery: namely, that hate speech, malicious lies, attacks on democracy and other forms of expression are really dangerous and can cause considerable harm. There is, of course, nothing new about this insight. Mill said it a century and a half ago. Honest civil libertarians have long acknowledged it. We are seeing it happening in real time today. What is new is

---

23   Anthony Romero, We Can Uphold Free Speech and Hold President Trump Accountable, Jan. 11, 2021.

the conclusion some of these current censors have drawn from the old insight: namely, that selective censorship is the answer. This, too, is as old as the Sedition Act of 1798, which one of the new censors actually cites as a model response to the "crisis of misinformation and its potential to undermine trust in elected officials."[24]

In this short book, I will describe the current regressive war against freedom of speech being waged by "progressives," social media moguls, university administrators, and other well-meaning but dangerous censors. I will assess the role of the Trump presidency in energizing this backlash against basic liberties and put it in the broader context of how anti-Trump zealots weaponized, distorted and weakened constitutional protections in an effort to "get" Trump by any means. I will focus on censorship by private social media, as well as by public institutions. I will also explore and assess the changing attitudes toward the value of free speech. Finally, I will propose steps that can be taken to defend, reclaim, and strengthen freedom of speech and other basic liberties that are under attack.

L) Non-Governmental Censorship

Because the current attacks against freedom of speech are coming in large part from powerful *non-governmental*

---

24 Katlyn Marie Carter, What the 1798 Sedition Act got right – and what it means today, *Washington Post*, Jan. 14, 2021

institutions—such as social and other media, universities, publishers, lawyers, bar associations, and other private "influencers" and shapers of public opinion —they cannot be fought exclusively in the courts of law or in legislative assemblies. They must be fought primarily in the courts of public opinion. Private parties who would deny freedom of speech to others have their own freedom of speech, which includes the right to advocate and even impose censorship, as long as they don't employ state action— governmental assistance— in doing so. That is why the selective censorship currently being imposed by Facebook, Twitter, YouTube, and other giant social and print media is so difficult to combat. The last thing principled supporters of free speech want to see is governmental control over private media companies. We want these companies to remain free to exercise their First Amendment rights and decide what to publish and not publish. We just don't like the way they are exercising their First Amendment rights to selectively censor others. We must oppose them in the marketplace of ideas and persuade them that they are violating the spirit of the First Amendment while hiding behind its legitimate protections.

There are some judicial and legislative initiatives that can be helpful in protecting freedom of speech on social media. These include limitations on the special exemptions accorded internet platforms under section 230 of the Communications Decency Act. These exceptions from defamations and other causes of action presuppose that these platforms do not exercise effective control over the content place on them by third parties, but that they simply post what is sent to them. Now that these internet providers are, in fact, exercising control and censoring speech based on lawful but controversial content, there have been proposals to limit or even eliminate their exemption from defamation and other legal remedies. Some have argued that private platforms that take advantage of governmentally authorized exemptions become state actors subject to the First Amendment, because the governmental exemption facilitates censorship. Others claim that when social media succumb to governmental pressure to censure, they too become state actors. These issues, and others, are currently being litigated and may produce judicial decisions in the near future.

There are also private efforts by non-government actors to address the problems faced by internet platforms that are understandably concerned about becoming facilitators of hate speech, dangerous falsehoods, and violence. Recently, Facebook announced that in an effort to create objective, neutral and consistent standards, it would appoint a panel of experts from around the world to assess its criteria for allowing or censoring speech on its platform. The panel includes winners of prestigious awards, former judges, law professors, literary figures, and others with valued reputations. This bevy of platonic guardians would decide whether something could be posted, whether it should be accompanied with a cautionary label, or whether it should be totally banned.

It's an interesting idea, and a potentially constructive component of any approach to addressing the accusations that Facebook and other social media are biased against conservatives and in favor of liberals and progressives. But it is a double-edged sword.

The positive edge is that it places the decision-making in the hands of a more diverse, politically balanced, and presumably objective group of wise men and women, who will assure that any censorship is based on neutral standards of general applicability across the political and ideological spectrum—"-ism equity."

The negative edge of the sword is that it legitimates a regime of private censorship, even if benign, by social media platforms. Because it will likely reduce the likelihood of overtly partisan censorship, this process makes subtler forms of nuanced censorship seem acceptable. Moreover, it sets a dangerous precedent. Today's guardians may be neutral—though at least one of them who I know is a zealous anti-Trump partisan.[25] But in the future, these guardians may shift right or left. Or they may have hidden biases based on identity politics and other forms of political correctness. Once

---

25 Stanford Professor Pamela Karlan had to apologize for remarks she made about Trump's young son during President Trump's first impeachment, in which she testified in favor of impeachment, *Wash. Post*, December 5, 2019.

the concept of a board of censors is approved and widely accepted, it can become a model for other social media, as well as for a wide array of other institutions. The very idea of platonic guardians telling us what is "truth," what is "false-hood," what we can be trusted to read without commentary, and what is too dangerous for us to be exposed to, is a potential prescription for Big Brother, Big Sister, or at the very least small siblings who may grow into big censors.

This is not to say that we should discourage innovative private, as well as public, efforts to ameliorate the problems of today's media censorship. It is to say that we should be cautious about approving short-term solutions that pose long term dangers.

M) The Spirit of Liberty

In the end, the spirit of liberty—as Justice Learned Hand wisely observed – "lies in the hearts of men and women." And when "It dies there, no constitution, no law, no court" can do much to save it.[26] During the past several years, the spirit of liberty has been weakened by a growing acceptance of censorship, especially among young people on the left. It must not be allowed to die, or be killed by men and women "of zeal, well meaning, but without understanding."[27]

---

26 Learned Hand, Spirit of Liberty (1944).
27 Olmstead v. U.S., 277 U.S. 438 (1928) (Brandeis, J. dissenting).

The important question is not so much whether one supports freedom of speech in the abstract—most Americans do. The question is whether one prioritizes free speech over other values when they come in conflict, as they often do. The American Civil Liberties Union used to prioritize free speech, but in recent years, they have placed a higher value on other progressive causes, such as a woman's right to choose, racial, gender, and sexual-orientation equality, immigration, the environment and other progressive values, and especially opposition to President Trump (which has increased their contributions dramatically).[28] They fail to understand that if freedom of speech is compromised in the interest of promoting these other values, those values will suffer as well. The open marketplace of ideas is an essential prerequisite to advocating the progressive agenda (as well as the regressive agenda).

We must struggle to protect our freedoms by persuading our fellow Americans that censorship against anyone inevitably leads to censorship against everyone. Free speech for me but not for thee is the first step down the road to free speech for neither me nor thee. We must heed the classic message of the anti-Nazi Lutheran Minister Martin Niemöller: "First they came for the socialists, and I did not

---

28   Larry Neumeister & Michael Sisak, A.C.L.U. Is Seeing A Trump-Era Surge in Members and Donations, Feb. 12, 2017, available at https://apnews.com/article/1dbcc13bc0104edaabb1d55c13483101

speak out—because I was not a socialist. Then they came for the trade unionists, and I did not speak out—because I was not a trade unionist. Then they came for the Jews, and I did not speak out because I was not a Jew. Then they came for me, and there was no one left to speak for me."

The great iconoclast H.L. Mencken put it more pithily: "The trouble about fighting for human freedom is that you have to spend much of your life defending sons of bitches: for oppressive laws are always aimed at them originally, and oppression must be stopped in the beginning if it is to be stopped at all."

We must defend the rights of others if we want others to defend our rights—and even if others refuse to defend our rights. Because their rights are our rights!

The struggle for free speech never stays won. It must be fought every day and against every enemy—right, left, and center—in the court of public opinion.

Ever since the rejection of the Sedition Act by President Thomas Jefferson, Americans have shown rhetorical support for freedom of speech pursuant to the First Amendment. Not all Americans have always practiced what they preach with regard to freedom of speech. Over the generations, many have found justifications—excuses—for accepting free speech for me but not for thee. But until the last decade, there have been few attacks on the very concept of free speech itself. Now some on the hard left seek to justify—indeed to proclaim—the virtue of selective censorship in the interest of higher values, such as anti-racism, anti-sexism, and other progressive agendas.[29] The voices of these censors must not be silenced. They, too, must be heard. Those of us who defend free speech must not censor the censors. We must not accept their approach to closing down the marketplace of ideas. Nor should we become disagreeable about our disagreements. They make an important point when they protest against racism, hate and untruth. We make an even more important point when we defend freedom of speech against their short-sighted zealousness. We must respond to their well-intentioned but dangerous views on their merits and demerits. We must persuade open-minded people of the virtues of free speech and of the vices of selective censorship. We must defeat their ideas in the open marketplace. We must convince doubters that the road to censorship hell is paved with good intentions. We must lead them down a better road—a road with its own pitfalls, dangers, and harmful outcomes, but a road that is far better than the roadblocks of censorship.

We must be prepared to respond to the new arguments of the new censors—the "good" censors—with our own new and better answers, rooted in old and enduring verities. We must enter the marketplace and engage.

---

29   See generally Alan M. Dershowitz, *Cancel Culture*, Hot Books, 2020.

Just as every generation has its own music, fashion, and tastes, so, too, does every generation have its own priorities based on its experiences. But the enduring value of freedom of expression—without which there will be no freedom to choose music or fashion—should not be a matter of generational taste or preference. To paraphrase Lillian Hellman's response to McCarthyism: We must not and should not cut our collective "conscience to fit this year's"—or this generation's—"fashions." Ecclesiastes observed that "to everything there is a season," but he also reminded us that some enduring values transcend generations and "abideth forever." Freedom of expression must be among those enduring values.

In the end, our modest goal is to persuade the nay-sayers that freedom of speech, like democracy itself, is the least worst alternative in a world filled with risks and dangers on all sides. We must accept the burden of proving to a skeptical world that free speech is the lifeblood of democracy—that, without it, democracy cannot survive.[30] I willingly take on that burden.

Hence this book.

---

30 The value of free speech transcends even democracy. It would be essential even in a monarchy or aristocracy. Democracy cannot exist without freedom of expression, but freedom of expression can exist even in the absence of democracy. In their brief advocating the second impeachment and disqualification of Donald Trump, the managers make the mistake of arguing that "the First Amendment exists to protect our democratic system." In reality, it exists to protect every system of governance.

CHAPTER 1

The Events Leading Up to the Free-Speech Crisis: Was the Election Fair?

———

In the run-up to the 2020 election, I wrote a series of op-eds that dealt with free speech and fair elections. I predicted the possibility of violence in reaction to the election. What I said back then is as relevant today as when I wrote them.

A. Are We Ready for a Wave of Violence After the Election?

We must prepare now for the possibility of violence following the election this fall. If it turns out to be a close or contested election, extremists from both sides may likely use it as an excuse to riot and attack. This will not be a repeat of the 2000 election, when the disputes were ultimately resolved by the Supreme Court in a controversial decision along partisan lines. The loser accepted it and told his followers to do the same.

But in this election, the candidates are not George Bush and Al Gore, and the country is not what it was twenty years ago. This is a very different and far more dangerous time. We are a much more divided nation. Violence is in the air in many of our cities and has received a degree of legitimacy from people on both sides who should know better. We are not prepared for a possibility of dangerous reactions to an election that may seem unfair to people on one side or the other based on the outcome.

A perfect storm may be just over the horizon, if not already here in several respects. There is a pandemic that could worsen by November, difficulties for voting, high unemployment, continued racial protests that sometimes devolve into violence, deadly wildfires out west that each side blames on the other, rabid hatred of opposition candidates fueled by the media, and criticism and defunding of the police, which disincentivizes many officers from aggressively preventing or responding to violence.

There is reported unwillingness of several district attorneys to prosecute violent protesters with whose goals they might agree, fear among some political leaders of alienating the Black Lives Matter movement, abuse of the justice system for partisan advantage, broad distrust of government institutions and officials, as well as of the media, and several Americans with foul moods caused by isolation and other difficulties.

Such components of a perfect storm do not guarantee that there will be violence, but they surely increase the likelihood that the extremists, and perhaps even people who up to now have not engaged in violence, may very well take to the streets instead of, or in addition to, the courts. Both sides are gearing up for potential legal battles, as they should do. But we should also be preparing for potential street battles this fall.

Preventing and responding to violence has to be our bipartisan concern. Neither side benefits from reckless actions, and both sides benefit from stability and the rule of law. Only the most extremist elements of both sides, who desire revolution rather than evolution, benefit from violence. Yet there are those in both sides who subtly apply a different standard to violence based on its source. Some on the left "understand," if not justify, violence against perceived racial injustice and police misconduct. Some on the right "understand," if not justify, violence against those who would tear down our nation, destroy statues, and attack our police.

Both are wrong. There has to be one standard of condemning violence, regardless of the source or reason. Our Constitution and our laws provide peaceful remedies to wrongs, regardless of the source or reason. Further, the rule of violence is simply the antithesis of the rule of law. Both parties and candidates have to declare they condemn all violent reactions to the election while supporting proper legal remedies. The Justice Department has to coordinate with state and local law enforcement officials. Attorney General William Barr has to immediately establish a bipartisan task force to anticipate and prepare for any violence after the election.

The key to preventing violence is bipartisan actions and words. If violence is stoked even subtly by either side, then it will persist and escalate. We all have a stake in preventing violence, since its targets tend to be random. In the riots and vandalism of these recent months, the victims have included minority store owners and others who had just been in the wrong place at the wrong time. When violence spreads, it provokes more violence, as we have seen during this unrest. We all are potential victims.

The time to take action is now, before the outcome in the election this fall is known, and while we still can speak out and take key measures against violence in a bipartisan manner. Once the election is over, and especially if it produces that kind of uncertain outcome reminiscent of 2000, it will be past this deadline for a united front against violence that may almost certainly be perceived as supporting one side or the other.

What is at stake is nothing less than the rule of law which benefits us all, regardless of party affiliation. We must preserve it against mob violence, whatever its source or reason. If we are to preserve the rule of law after the election, we must take action before the voting begins.

B. Our Shrill Nation has Lost Ability to Debate

The first presidential debate of 2020 marked the culmination of the growing inability of our nation's leaders — and indeed its citizens — to conduct reasoned and respectful debates about public matters. The concept of disagreeing without being disagreeable is out the window, and with it our long history of polite public discourse.

I love debating. I grew up in a household in which everything was debated.

I was captain of my high school and college debate teams.

I won moot court competitions in law school. I debated William J. Buckley on television.

I won a series of debates on intelligence Square.

Recently however, I have found it increasingly difficult to find debating partners.

I used to debate Jeffrey Toobin on CNN. But then CNN banned me, because they were apparently dissatisfied with the outcomes of our debates. The same is true of MSNBC.

I used to write op-eds for *The New York Times*.

No more, because virtually all of their op-eds are one sided and predictable.

I was not surprised, therefore, at the first presidential debate. It did not break new ground; it was simply an inevitable culmination of a movement over the years away from reasoned and respectful dialogue.

When I came to Harvard in 1964 to begin teaching, debates were common on the campus.

I participated in many of them.

Today, there are few, if any, real debates on many college campuses. In their place, there are demonstrations, shouting matches, accusations, cancellations, and bumper stickers.

Instead of providing opposing points of view to "politically correct" positions, universities are providing psychological counselling to those who are frightened when exposed to contrary views.

Thus, they want safe spaces for their ideas, while denying their opponents even the opportunity to express differing views.

This is the world in which the recent presidential debate took place.

Why should anyone be surprised at the absence of civility, respect for opposing views and the need for real dialogue?

That's not the world we live in today, and that's not the world our children and grandchildren will live in if what is occurring on university campuses today continues to move into the mainstream.

We see the same kind of abusive personal attacks now in judicial confirmation hearings, especially for Supreme Court justices. No sooner did the president nominate a controversial judge — Amy Coney Barrett — than a Boston university professor attacked her for adopting two Black children, suggesting that she might have been motivated by colonialists' or white supremacists' ideas.

I am sure his views will be widely praised on campuses, despite their cruelty and ignorance. When Justice Brett Kavanaugh was nominated, the attack on him focused on conduct he was accused of engaging in, but veraciously denied, when he was a high school teenager.

We can expect even worse in future confirmation hearings.

It may well be true that President Trump has set a poor example in his choice of words in attacking enemies, but he's simply replicating the tone and style of much of what passes today as dialogue on college campuses, social media, and even mainstream television and radio.

We are a shrill nation, more interested in making points than making sense. We do not respect our opponents right to respond to their arguments on their merits or demerits;

instead we insult them, demean them, attack their motives, and accuse them of racism, sexism, homophobia and every other -ism under the sun. We saw that in the presidential debate and it did not surprise me.

There is much to criticize in the substance of that particular debate, but that is not the point of this article, which is about how the debate was conducted, rather than what was said—and not said.

It will only get worse, regardless of who is elected president, because it began, especially on university campuses and in the media, well before President Trump entered the Oval Office, and because and it will continue after he leaves, whether this January or four years hence. It has become part of our culture, and cultures don't change with elections. The problem is deeper than any one person and more pervasive than any one debate.

Americans don't trust anyone. They distrust politicians, the media, and now even the Supreme Court. There are no more Walter Cronkites, Eli Wiesels, or other principled leaders whom everyone respects, regardless of party, race, or identity. Hatred is rampant. Intolerance is the norm. Next comes violence. It is inevitable when political opponents are dehumanized. We must change this culture today if we are to leave our children a better tomorrow.

C. Don't Expect Perfection in the Election

The 2020 presidential election will be imperfect. There will be some voter fraud. There will be some voter suppression. There will be mistakes, late ballots, unreadable mail-ins, and other imperfections. That is the nature of modern elections—even without foreign efforts to interfere.

We must do all we can to minimize over- or under-counting votes. We must also recognize that in an imperfect world with imperfect voting mechanisms, the end result will not be a perfect representation of the intent of American voters.

Nor will this be our first imperfect election. In 2000, George W. Bush was elected president by the tiniest margin—fewer than 600 votes in the state of Florida. Having been part of the legal team challenging that result, I have absolutely no doubt that more—many more—Floridians intended to vote for Al Gore than for George W. Bush. In Palm Beach County alone, hundreds of votes were accidentally cast for Pat Buchanan because of the illegal and confusing butterfly ballot. Had those votes and others, clearly intended for Gore, been counted for him, Bush may well have lost Florida by a decisive number and the case would never have ended up in the United States Supreme Court, which improperly stopped the recount in a 5-4 vote along party lines.

Going back further in time, many experts still wonder about the validity of John F. Kennedy's victories in several primaries as well as in the general election. Both Nixon and Gore eventually conceded defeat and allowed for a peaceful transition of power.

In the 19th century, there were several contested elections, including some that were decided by corrupt bargains. Things have actually gotten better over the years, especially with the enfranchisement of many more voters and with improvements in voter security. But, of course, the more voters we have, the greater the chances of imperfection. That is the price we pay for the goal of universal suffrage.

In the bad old days when only property-owning white males voted, it was easier to keep track of the relatively small voter pool.

There will always be some proper votes that are not counted and some improper votes that are. We should try to minimize both. But as a matter of policy and of law, we should always err on the side of inclusion rather than exclusion. Better a few improper votes be counted than many proper votes be discounted. Historically, there has been far more voter suppression than voter fraud, and the suppression has disproportionately affected minority voters. So the emphasis should be on eliminating voter suppression, while minimizing voter fraud.

To be sure, there is the risk that counting even a few improper votes could determine the outcome of an election, but the risk is even greater that leaving many proper votes uncounted can determine the outcome. That is plainly what happened in 2000, when voter suppression—both deliberate and inadvertent—skewed the votes away from the Democratic candidate in Florida.

When the polls close in this election, there will be complaints from both sides. Democrats will claim voter suppression. Republicans will claim voter fraud. Each side will have points to score. They will be able to demonstrate their claims anecdotally and perhaps statistically. One or both will surely seek relief from the courts, particularly if the election is very close in swing states. But in considering these claims, the courts should understand that perfection is impossible and that both law and policy should err on the side of inclusion rather than exclusion.

Voters themselves can reduce imperfections on both sides. Be persistent. Overcome efforts to discourage you. Be careful. Don't give the other side an excuse to invalidate your vote. Vote early. And most important: VOTE. The major cause of imperfect voting is self-suppression: eligible voters who simply don't cast a ballot. Don't be a cause of imperfection in the 2020 election. Vote.

D. AOC Has Finally Crossed the Line

[On October 9, 2020, I criticized Congresswoman Alexandria Ocasio-Cortez for sounding a "dog whistle to violent organizations." She and others on the hard left, as well as the hard right, continue to do so.]

Rep. Alexandria Ocasio-Cortez, D-N.Y., the young folk hero commonly known as AOC, has crossed the line from radicalism to anti-Americanism and anti-decency.

Tellingly, she now operates through an organization called *Jacobin*, named after French revolutionaries who descended into barbarity and mass murder.

Indeed, the word terrorism arises from the "reign of terror" of which they were an important part.

By identifying with such violent radicals, AOC sounds a dog whistle to violent organizations such as Antifa and others on the Hard-Left who want revolution, not evolution.

AOC's most recent manifestation of support for violence is her campaign to "defund the police." This is what her most recent ad, "From: Ocasio Cortez via Jacobin," says: "Right now, most major cities in America are channeling huge war chests of money into police departments . . ."

That is a blatant falsehood.

Police men and women around the country suffer from extremely low pay. They are working people who put their lives at risk every day to defend the most vulnerable among us.

Law enforcement needs more funding, not *defunding*.

More funding would pay for better police training, better non-lethal weapons, better community policing and better protection for vulnerable victims, many of whom live in minority communities.

AOC and her fellow revolutionaries believe that today's world is "based on racist, violent policing . . ."

This paints with far too broad a brush. I know many police officers, FBI, secret service, and other members of law enforcement. I am generally on the opposite side of them in the courtroom.

But the vast, vast majority of them are honest, decent, hardworking people who have devoted their lives to protecting the rest of us, and most especially those most subject to victimization in high-crime areas.

The last thing they ever want to do is fire their service revolvers at anyone, most especially anyone innocent.

They are not murderers, as AOC characterizes them, calling the tragic death of Breonna Taylor a "murder," despite evidence that the police fired in response to a shot from her boyfriend that hit and nearly killed an officer.

Such bigotry against police officers and such generalizations about racism are to be condemned by all decent people.

AOC's indecency was also recently manifested when she was invited by a pro-peace left-wing Jewish organization to commemorate the death of Israel's great peace-maker, Yitzhak Rabin.

Rabin was assassinated by a hard-right extremist who opposed Rabin's efforts to make peace with the Palestinians and to recognize a Palestinian state. AOC originally accepted an invitation to appear at the event, but after being pressured by virulent anti-Zionists, who believe that Israel has no right to exist as the nation-state of the Jewish people, she backed out.

AOC's cowardly decision not to stand up to anti-Semitic, anti-Israel bigotry is being applauded by fellow bigots on the hard left.

When AOC was first elected, I urged leaders of the Jewish community to reach out to her in order to educate her about Israel's history and its enormous contribution to the well-being of the planet.

No country in history has ever done so much good for humanity in so short a period of time as in the seventy-two years since Israel has come into existence. Efforts were made to reach out to her to invite her to visit Israel to meet with Jewish leaders on the left, and most recently, to join in honoring Israel's peace martyr, Yitzhak Rabin.

She has rebuffed all efforts to build bridges to the pro-Israel community — even its most left-wing members.

Although she has been deliberately vague about her position with regard to Israel, it now seems evidently clear that she does not recognize Israel's right to exist and to live in peace as the nation-state of the Jewish people.

If she did, she would not have refused to attend the pro-peace memorial to Rabin.

AOC has now crossed the line from radicalism to bigotry, from extremism to intolerance, and from ignorance to willful mendacity. AOC is no longer a friend of liberalism, of mainstream Judaism, or of basic decency. She is an enemy whose bigotry must be confronted at every turn and whose lies must be responded to with truth.

E. Can President Trump Win his Election Challenges in Court?

[Following President Trump's defeat in the election, his legal team brought lawsuits challenging the election. In an article on November 9, 2020, I explained why these challenges were unlikely to succeed, and I called for Trump to concede once his legal options were exhausted. He refused.]

Lawyers on cable news are debating whether President Trump can reverse his electoral fortunes in court. Rather than reasonable legal analyses from experts, we are hearing mostly wishful thinking from partisans. Those who want Trump to win tell the public that he may win. Those who want him to lose assure the public that he stands no chance in court.

The great Justice Oliver Wendell Holmes defined the role of lawyers as predicting, in fact, what the courts will decide. So here is my objective and independent prediction as to how the courts will likely resolve the number of challenges brought by Trump and his lawyers.

He could win his case in Pennsylvania about ballots mailed before the end of the election but received over the next three days. Justice Samuel Alito, who oversees the federal circuit that includes Pennsylvania, has signaled Supreme Court interest in that issue by ordering all of these ballots to be counted separately, then segregated. The Pennsylvania secretary of state was doing this, but the order from Alito made clear that there are at least some others who could be ready to discount those votes.

Article Two provides that state legislatures determine rules for selecting members of the Electoral College. But it was the Pennsylvania high court, not the legislature, that extended time for receiving and counting mailed ballots by three days. It may have been a sensible decision in light of the coronavirus and problems with delivery. According to lawyers for Trump, the state high court lacked the authority to change the rules that mailed ballots have to be received before the end of the election.

Twenty years ago, in the Supreme Court decision in George Bush versus Al Gore, the majority voted along strictly partisan lines to stop the count ordered by the Florida high court. That decision had been based in part on Article Two. It is likely, therefore, that the even more partisan current Supreme Court might well side with Trump over this issue.

The issue remains whether a decision in favor of Trump would alter the outcome for Pennsylvania. If Joe Biden has won the state by a margin in excess of the challenged votes, then a victory for Trump on Article Two grounds is pointless, as Biden would still carry the state. If the Supreme Court is uncertain whether a decision to discount the challenged votes would change the outcome, it could decline to intervene. There will be cases in Michigan, Nevada, Arizona, Georgia, and perhaps others. Such lawsuits will be even more difficult for Trump and his team.

The lawsuit in Pennsylvania is a "wholesale" challenge to a large number of votes counted in violation of state legislation. That lawsuit is based on the matter of constitutional law, so it does not need evidence or a trial. It was already before the Supreme Court, which was divided over the issue. All that is necessary is further briefings and a final decision.

The lawsuits in other states are "retail" in nature. They involve objections to particular votes, specific practices, and local rules. For them to prevail would take a presentation of evidence, which would likely be contested by the other side. These challenges will be messy and will therefore take some time. In order to prevail, they would have to show that there were enough disputed votes to make a difference in the final outcome of the election in a given state. That will not be an easy task to do.

For Trump to reverse the outcome of the election, he needs to prove that there were enough invalid votes in enough states to win the 270 electoral votes for victory. Turning around the results in any particular state, even in Pennsylvania, will not do that. He must prove a difference in several states. That depends on which states, if any, he wins in court and then how many electoral votes they have. It is a daunting battle. For 2000, all Bush had to do was to focus on Florida, and he could do that as a matter of wholesale constitutional law rather than retail evidentiary challenges. That decision serves as only a partial precedent for all the current cases.

Challenging election results, even with demanding recounts or bringing lawsuits, is part of democracy, when the ultimate loser notes the results and concedes defeat, as Gore did back in 2000. Trump and his lawyers should not be condemned, as they have been by many, for pursuing the lawsuits. Once the remedies are exhausted, the American way demands that the loser concedes with the final mandated outcome.

F. Will Warnock's Anti-Israel Views Determine Who Controls the Senate?

[The Presidential election, though the most important, was not the only crucial vote. Control of the Senate turned on the double election in Georgia. The Democratic candidate had a problematic past, about which I wrote. He eventually changed some of his most troubling positions and won a narrow victory.]

Control of the United States Senate may turn on whether the Democratic candidate, Reverend Raphael Warnock, defeats the Republican incumbent, Kelly Loeffler, in the January 5th Georgia runoff. As a liberal Democrat, I would rather see a Warnock victory that could create a 50-50 tie in the Senate, capable of being broken by future vice president Kamala Harris. But as a strong supporter of Israel, I am deeply concerned about the fact that Reverend Warnock signed a statement in 2019 and gave a sermon in 2018 that demonstrated strong antagonism to the nation-state of the Jewish people.

Some have deliberately distorted Warnock's anti-Israel views in an attempt to garner Jewish support for Warnock. For example, here is the way *The Forward* described the content of the letter:

Warnock recently came under fire from some Atlanta Jews after Jewish Insider noted that he signed onto a 2019 statement from a group of Christian clergy that visited Israel and the West Bank that likened the "heavily militarization of the West Bank" to "the military occupation of Namibia by apartheid, South Africa." The statement specifies that its signatories "support a two-state solution."

The Forward then says "Jewish political observers disagree with the notion that Warnock is not a strong supporter of Israel."

In order to assess the accuracy of the foregoing description, let us look at the text of the letter itself.

The letter accuses Israel of "state-sanctioned violence in the form of detention, interrogation, teargassed [sic], beatings, forced confessions and death." It characterizes the separation barrier that has saved so many lives as "ever-present physical walls that wall in Palestinians in a political wall reminiscent of the Berlin Wall." Never once does the letter mention why the separation barrier was necessary. The word terrorism never once appears in the letter.

The letter goes on to talk about the Gaza Strip and alleges "excessive use of force by Israel to subjugate the people in collective punishment of whole population [sic] in the debilitating confinement that renders Gaza as one big densely populated prison." There is not a single mention of the thousands of rockets fired from Gaza that have killed, injured, and traumatized Israelis living within the 1967 borders. Not a word is said about the terror tunnels dug from Gaza to the outskirts of Israel Kibbutzim to murder innocent Israeli men, women, and children.

The letter purports to describe the "laws of segregation that allow one thing for the Jewish people and another for the Palestinians." There are different rules for Israelis and non-Israeli residents of the West Bank, but they are not based on religion. Palestinians who live in Israel—whether Muslim or Christian—are full citizens with equal protection under Israeli laws. There are no roads for "Jews only," as is often alleged. Because of the threat of terrorism against Israelis, there are secure roads for Israeli citizens, but Muslim and Christian citizens of Israel have full access to those roads.

The letter applauds the Palestinian Authority for its "conscious decision to forgo armed solutions to the conflict." No mention is made of the "pay-to-slay" policy of the Palestinian Authority that encourages and rewards terrorism and that has been condemned by every American administration and by Congress.

The letter also criticized the United States' decision to recognize Jerusalem as "Israel's official capital," without mentioning that every American administration since the 1990s pledged to do it.

The letter condemns "the increasing hardening of the hearts of the Israeli powers that be," without mentioning Israel's offers to end the occupation of the West Bank and establish a Palestinian state—all of which the Palestinian Authority rejected on numerous occasions.

The letter's authors pray for an end to "weapons sales," which would mean a weakened Israel subject to attack by Iran and its surrogates, as well as by terrorists.

Finally, the letter expresses support for "utilizing economic pressure as a means of bringing recalcitrant dominant forces to the negotiating table." This remark fails to recognize that Israel has extended an open offer to the Palestinian Authority leadership to sit down at the negotiation table and that it has been the Palestinians who have refused to negotiate.

I urge everyone to read the entire letter and listen to the entire sermon, because not only are their words reflective of a strong anti-Israel bias and one-sided criticism of Israel, but their tone is biased in the extreme. For those who argue that Warnock merely signed on to a group letter that may not have reflected his own views, please listen to his sermon, which accuses Israel of "shoot[ing] down unarmed Palestinians sisters and brothers like birds of prey." This is a mendacious blood libel, pure and simple. You wouldn't know that from reading the misleading description of the letter and sermon in *The Forward*. Nor would you know that Warnock is an admirer of Reverend Jeremiah Wright and a defender of the anti-American and anti-Semitic sermon that President Obama condemned.

So it is important for everyone who is considering voting for Reverend Warnock to read the letter and listen to the sermon in their entirety. I have done so and I find it difficult to support anyone who has such animosity toward Israel. Nor can I believe that anyone who holds such views can be characterized as "a strong supporter of Israel."

I am prepared to change my mind about Reverend Warnock, but only if he changes his mind about Israel. The mere fact that after announcing his candidacy, he renounced support for BDS and mouthed some talking points about Israel's security (see his recent op-ed, "I Stand With Israel") is not enough for me. I want to know what he really believes and, more importantly, how he will vote.

The last thing the Democratic Party needs is yet another prominent politician who harbors negative views about America's most reliable ally, Israel. I hope Reverend Warnock will reconsider his past mistakes and express views that allow liberal Democrats like me, who are also strong supporters of Israel, to support him in his bid to become a United States senator. I genuinely want to be able to support Reverend Warnock and a Democratic Senate, and I truly hope he can convince me and the voters of Georgia that he really does "stand with Israel."

Chapter 2

Impeachment and Censorship for a Speech that Is Constitutionally Protected by the First Amendment

———

After President Trump's provocative speech of January 6, 2021 and the attack on the capitol that followed, the House of Representatives impeached Trump for the Second Time. I wrote a series of articles critical of both the speech and the impeachment.

A. Our Constitution Has Passed this Difficult Stress Test

[On the day after the outrageous and unlawful assault on the Capitol, I wrote about the challenge posed by this riot and how we survived it and restored the rule of law.]

Our Constitution was subjected to a difficult stress test this week. For the first time in modern history, violent protesters breached the Capitol and entered the chambers and offices of members of Congress, threatening lives and destroying property. Deaths and injuries occurred.

The primary fault lies with the protesters themselves. However, there was more than enough blame to go around here. The police should have been better prepared for the rioters, who were urged by President Trump to go to the Capitol. It was inevitable that some may break the law, trespass on federal property, and perhaps engage with acts of violence.

But it was a mistake to cast blame on officials who exercised their right to object to an election at rallies and in Congress. The First Amendment and the speech and debate clause of the Constitution are crucial elements of our democracy. Their limits were tested by the remarks Trump made with his supporters and by those of Senator Ted Cruz and others.

Neither the First Amendment nor the speech and debate clause are limited to words and rhetoric with which we concur; they were designed to permit controversial speech, or even dangerous speech, that remains within the constraints of the law. The remarks this week, while disturbing and concerning, were well within those constraints.

To hold speakers accountable for violence that ensued would endanger our rights protected by the Constitution. Free speech is not free. Illegal actions, including violence, often follow incendiary words. When French publication *Charlie Hebdo* deliberately published cartoons that the staff knew would be offensive to Muslims, its editors should have anticipated the possibility of heated reactions. When the violence did in fact occur, some blamed the publication and tried to limit free speech.

The same holds true across history, as union leaders, civil rights activists, and so many others have made remarks they knew or should have known risked violence. I have defended such agitators over the last half century and will continue to do so. Efforts to constrain free speech based on this possibility of violence would do more enduring harm to our fundamental rights than those rioters themselves did with all their chaos.

Thomas Jefferson addressed this on the eve of the 25th anniversary of the Declaration of Independence. He tackled the notion that a minister whose sermon incited some violence should be punished. He argued against that action, calling for only the punishment of those who committed the violence. The Framers of our First Amendment understood that free speech is not free. It carries with it significant risk. Those risks came to fruition in the terrible assault on the Capitol. But the Constitution has endured similar assaults, and it will endure this one as well. Some critics have called for the invocation of the 25th Amendment to

replace Trump for his last two weeks in office. It was created to replace a president unable to perform duties due to
medical incapacity. It was not intended as a substitute for
impeachment or to stop a controversial president from fin-
ishing a term. This is unrelated, and efforts to use it imperil
the rule of law.

The same is true of efforts for the second impeachment
of Trump. Nothing that he did, regardless of the merits
or demerits, comes within the criteria for impeachment
and removal. Some believe that while there is no chance
of removing him, he should face impeachment, since
Democrats have the votes in the House for impeachment,
but not the votes within the Senate for removal. That is an
exercise in power rather than in legality.

The Constitution was subjected to a difficult stress
test this week. But the Constitution, with its system of
checks and balances, passed this test. The debate resumed
in Congress, and the resolutions challenging the election
rightly failed. Trump even wrote, "There will be an orderly
transition on January 20." Further, several of the rioters will
be charged and convicted. No compromises were made, at
least not yet, with our basic liberties. So the bad news is that
violence occurred on the grounds of our Capitol for several
hours. But the great news is that our nation survived.

B. Impeachment Over Protected Speech Would Harm the Constitution

[On January 12 2021, I explained that President Trump had the constitutional *right* to deliver his speech, but that he was *wrong* to do so.]

Whatever one may think of President Trump's speech last Wednesday—I personally found it deeply upsetting—one thing is clear: It was fully protected by the First Amendment. Nothing the president said constituted unprotected "incitement," as narrowly defined by the Supreme Court over nearly a century of decisions. His volatile words plainly fell on the side of political "advocacy," which is protected speech.

In the leading case of *Brandenburg v. Ohio*, a unanimous Supreme Court ruled that even advocacy of the use of force is constitutionally protected, unless it is specifically "directed to inciting or producing imminent lawless action." In subsequent decisions, the courts have narrowly defined "incitement" to exclude the kind of speech delivered by President Trump. Although he used fighting words, he urged his listeners to march to the capitol and protest "peacefully and patriotically." He *invited*, not *incited*. His speech—disturbing as it may have been—is within the core protection of political speech.

If that is correct, then the following question arises: whether the constitutional criteria for impeachment—"treason, bribery or other high crimes and misdemeanors"—can plausibly be understood to encompass constitutionally protected expression; that is, speech that could not constitutionally be made criminal under the First Amendment's mandate that "Congress shall make no law ... abridging the freedom of speech." The constitutionally correct answer to that question is surely no.

So the article of impeachment Democrats introduced in Congress—which focuses on President Trump's speech that urged listeners to go to the Capitol—is unconstitutional. Impeaching President Trump on grounds that violate both the First Amendment and the impeachment clause would do more serious and enduring harm to our Constitution than the unlawful rioters did when they temporarily took over the Capitol building. These rioters did grave harm to the rule of law, but at the end of a long and difficult day, the rule of law prevailed. The Capitol was secured and Congress continued with its business, voting down what the rioters were demanding. Many of those who broke the law have been arrested and will be prosecuted and convicted for serious crimes including possibly homicide. But now, the Democratic leaders of Congress, and some Republicans, are threatening to take political steps that endanger the line carefully drawn by First Amendment jurisprudence between those who advocate unlawful conduct and those who commit it.

When the Supreme Court notoriously upheld the unconstitutional detention of more than 100,000 Americans of Japanese descent during World War Two, Justice Robert Jackson issued a memorable dissent that is relevant to our current situation. He acknowledged that the military order in question was "not apt to last longer than the military emergency." But Jackson argued that when it is "rationaliz[ed] to show that the Constitution sanctions such an order," the precedent "lies about like a loaded weapon ready for the hand of any authority that can bring forward a plausible claim of urgent need." The same would be true of an impeachment based on a constitutionally protected speech that caused several hours of inexcusable violence.

Defending the First Amendment does not require agreement with what the president said. I strongly disapprove of much of the content of his speech and wish he hadn't given it, but I stand with the defense of free speech attributed to Voltaire more than 200 years ago: "I disapprove of what you say, but I will defend to the death your right to say it."

The major criterion for this impeachment—"incitement to sedition"—has been misused throughout our history in efforts to suppress the advocacy of controversial speakers, including union leaders, civil rights activists, suffragettes, and other protesters and dissenters. It is an open-ended concept that can be expanded to cover many constitutionally protected protests. That is why the Supreme Court has repeatedly rejected efforts to circumvent the First Amendment by accusing advocates of "incitement," "sedition," "insurrection," "treason" and other loaded-but-vague phrases and words. Even when a speaker's advocacy is the "but for" cause of the resulting violence, the First Amendment protects it unless the speaker expressly incited the violence that immediately ensued. That is not what President Trump did.

Those who would compromise our hard-earned constitutional rights for short-term partisan expediency are ignoring the big picture. Weaponizing the Constitution as a political sword has consequences. Today it is being wielded against a Republican president. Tomorrow it may be wielded against a Democratic president. As Senator James N. Grimes warned during the impeachment trial of President Andrew Johnson, removing a president on grounds not specified in the Constitution would normalize "impeachment as part of future political machinery." That is what has been happening since the Republicans improperly impeached President Bill Clinton in 1998.

Even if those seeking to end President Trump's term by unconstitutional means are well intentioned, they must not be allowed to damage our Constitution. As Justice Louis Brandeis cautioned a century ago: "The greatest dangers to liberty lurk in insidious encroachment by men [and women] of zeal, well-meaning but without understanding."

President Trump has now called for an orderly transition of power. Democrats should not interfere with this transition by demanding a divisive two-step transfer— first to Vice President Pence for a few days and then to president-elect Biden—by means of an unconstitutional impeachment.

C. Trump Did Not Shout "Fire!"

[On January 15, 2021, I explained why the widely invoked "fire in the crowded theater" was not relevant to President Trump's speech]

Since President Donald Trump delivered his controversial tirade last Wednesday, pundits, politicians, professors and ordinary people have compared it to Justice Oliver Wendell Holmes Jr.'s famous example of unprotected speech:

The most stringent protection of free speech would not protect a man in falsely shouting fire in a theater, and causing a panic.

Shouting "Fire!" in a theater may well be the only juris-prudential analogy that has assumed the status of a folk argument. A prominent historian characterized it as "the most brilliantly persuasive expression that ever came from Holmes' pen." But in spite of its hallowed position in both the jurisprudence of the First Amendment and the arsenal of political discourse, it is and was an inapt analogy, even in the context in which it was originally offered. It has lately become—despite, or perhaps even because of, the fre-quency and promiscuousness of its invocation—little more than a caricature of logical argumentation. It should not be presented as a serious argument in the context of free-dom of speech, or in the context of impeaching President Trump.

The case that gave rise to the "Fire!"-in-a-crowded-theater analogy—*Schenck v. United States*—involved the prosecution of Charles Schenck, who was the gen-eral secretary of the Socialist Party in Philadelphia. In 1917 a jury found Schenck and Elizabeth Baer guilty of attempting to cause insubordination among soldiers who had been drafted to fight in the First World War. He had circulated leaflets urging draftees not to "submit to intimidation" by fighting in a war conducted on behalf of "Wall Street's chosen few." Schenck admitted that the intent of the pamphlets' "impassioned language" was to "influence" draftees to resist the draft. Nothing in the pamphlet suggested that the draftees should use unlawful or violent means to oppose conscription: "It called for measures, such as a petition for the repeal of the act," and an exhortation to exercise "your right to assert your opposition the draft."

Justice Holmes, citing the example of "shouting fire," upheld the convictions, ruling that the pamphlet created "a clear and present danger" of hindering the war effort.

But the example of shouting "Fire!" bore little relationship to the facts of the Schenck pamphlet, which contained a substantive political message. The pamphlet urged its draftee readers to *think* about the message and then—if they so choose—to act on it in a lawful and nonviolent way. The man who shouts "Fire!" in a crowded theater is neither sending a political message nor inviting his listener to think about what he has said and decide what to do in a rational, calculated manner. On the contrary, the message is designed to force action *without* contemplation. The message "Fire!" is directed not to the mind and the conscience of the listener, but rather, to his adrenaline and his feet. It is a stimulus to immediate *action*, not thoughtful reflection.

In that respect the shout of "Fire!" is not even speech, in any meaningful sense of the term. It is a *clang* sound—the equivalent of setting off a nonverbal alarm. Had Justice Holmes been more honest about his example, he would have said that freedom of speech does not protect a person who pulls a fire alarm in the absence of a fire. But that obviously would have been irrelevant to the case at hand. The proposition that pulling an alarm is not protected speech certainly leads to the conclusion that shouting the word *fire* is also not protected. But the core analogy is the nonverbal alarm, and the derivative example is the verbal shout. By cleverly substituting the derivative shout for the core alarm, Holmes made it possible, falsely, to analogize one set of words to another—as he could not have done if he had begun with the self-evident proposition that setting off an alarm bell is not free speech.

The analogy is thus not only inapt but insulting. Most Americans do not respond to political rhetoric with the same kind of automatic acceptance expected of schoolchildren responding to a fire drill. Not a single recipient of the Schenck pamphlet is known to have changed his mind after reading it. Indeed, one draftee, who appeared as a prosecution witness, was asked whether reading a pamphlet asserting that the draft law was unjust would make him "immediately decide that you must erase that law." Not surprisingly, he replied, "I do my own thinking." A theater goer would probably not respond similarly if asked how to react to a shout of "Fire!"

Another important reason why the analogy is inapt is that Holmes emphasizes the factual falsity of the shout "Fire!" The Schenck pamphlet, however, was not factually false. It contained political opinions and ideas about the causes of the war. As the Supreme Court said: "The First Amendment recognizes no such thing as a 'false' idea." Nor does it recognize false opinions about the causes of war, or about the truth or falsity of electoral claims.

A closer analogy to the facts of the Schenck case might have been provided by a person's standing outside a theater, offering the patrons a leaflet advising them that in his opinion the theater was structurally unsafe, and urging them not to enter but to complain to the building inspectors. That analogy, however, would not have served Holmes' argument for punishing Schenck. Holmes needed an analogy that would appear relevant to Schenck's political speech but that would invite the conclusion that censorship was appropriate.

Ironically, the "Fire!" analogy is all that survives from the Schenck case; the ruling itself is no longer good law.

Over the years, since that wrong-headed decision a century ago, proponents of censorship have maintained that many expressions are issues "just like" or "equivalent to" falsely shouting "Fire!" in a crowded theater, and ought to be banned. The analogy is generally invoked, often with self-satisfaction, as an absolute argument-stopper. It does, after all, claim the high authority of the great Justice Holmes. I have rarely heard it invoked in a convincing, or even particularly relevant, way. But that, too, can claim lineage from the great Holmes.

Some close analogies to shouting "Fire!" or setting an alarm are, of course, available: calling in a false bomb threat, dialing 911 and falsely describing an emergency, or making a loud, gun-like sound in the presence of the president.

Analogies are, by their nature, matters of degree. Some are closer to the core example than others. But any attempt to analogize political ideas in a pamphlet, or President Trump's recent inflammatory speech, to the very different act of shouting "Fire!" in a crowded theater, is either self-deceptive or self-serving.

President Trump told his listeners to march on the Capitol "peacefully and patriotically." Some didn't go to the Capitol; others went and protested peacefully; still others engaged in serious criminal behavior. None responded as if he had shouted "Fire!"

The government does, of course, have some arguably legitimate bases for suppressing speech, which bear no relationship to shouting "Fire!" It may ban the publication of nuclear-weapon codes, of information about troop movements, and the identity of undercover agents. It may criminalize extortion threats and conspiratorial agreements.

It may also prohibit speech that is specifically "directed to inciting or producing imminent lawless action," but it may not prohibit "advocacy"—as distinguished from incitement of such action. President Trump's speech is clearly protected under this standard. It certainly is not the same as "falsely shouting fire in a theater." So let's stop invoking this flawed, inept and insulting analogy.

D. Congress Broke Records on Impeachment of Donald Trump

[On January 14, 2021, shortly after the House once again impeached President Trump, I explained why this ill-conceived action violated six provisions of the Constitution]

First, it violated the First Amendment, which prohibits the government from abridging free speech. By impeaching Trump for free speech that was protected in the unanimous Supreme Court decision in the case of Brandenburg versus Ohio, the First Amendment was violated.

Second, the House violated the substantive impeachment criteria for the Constitution, which limits impeachment to "treason, bribery or other high crimes and misdemeanors." It cannot be a high crime or misdemeanor for a president to deliver remarks protected by the Constitution.

If Congress can pass no law abridging free speech, then it certainly cannot pass an article of impeachment that abridges the free speech of a president.

Third, it violated due process by handing the president and his legal team no opportunity to present a defense or to formally challenge the article of impeachment. This sets a precedent for any future president.

Fourth, by trying to put Trump on trial in the Senate after he leaves office, the House violated the provision that allows Congress to remove a sitting president and, only if the Senate decides to remove him by a vote, could it add the sanction for a future disqualification from running for office. Congress has no authority over any president once he leaves office. If Congress had the power to impeach a private citizen to prevent him from running in the future, it could claim jurisdiction over millions of Americans eligible to be candidates for president in 2024. This would be a perilous interpretation of the Constitution, which would allow the party in control of Congress to impeach a popular candidate and preclude him or her from running.

Fifth, if the Senate were to conduct a trial of a private citizen, including a former president, then it would violate both the spirit and the letter of the prohibition against bills of attainder. In Great Britain, Parliament had the authority to try kings, other officials, and private citizens. The Framers of the Constitution rejected that power of

Congress and also limited its trial jurisdiction to impeaching government officials only while they served in office and could be removed. To conduct a show trial of a past president would be in violation of the prohibition against bills of attainder.

Sixth, Congress voted in favor of the resolution calling on Vice President Mike Pence to violate the 25th Amendment of the Constitution by falsely claiming that Trump is unable to continue to perform his duties. It is clear that the Framers of the 25th Amendment had intended it to apply only to presidents disrupted by physical illnesses, such as a stroke, or by obvious mental incapacity, such as advanced Alzheimer's, or falling unconscious after having been shot. To call on the vice president to improperly invoke the 25th Amendment was to act in violation of the Constitution.

E. Why I Am Suing CNN

[Because I am a strong supporter of the First Amendment, some people asked why I was suing CNN for defaming me. I offered the following explanation.]

I love the First Amendment, I support the First Amendment, I have litigated cases defending the First Amendment. I have written and taught about the First Amendment. And I was a law clerk for the Supreme Court when it rendered its landmark decision in *New York*

Times v. Sullivan. But I also understand the limitations of the First Amendment. Freedom of speech is designed to promote the marketplace of ideas. It is not a license for giant media companies to deliberately and maliciously defame citizens, even public figures. So when CNN made a decision to doctor a recording so as to deceive its viewers into believing that I said exactly the opposite of what I actually said, that action was not protected by the First Amendment. Here is what CNN did.

I was asked to present the Constitutional argument against President Trump's impeachment and removal to the United States Senate this past January. For an hour and seven minutes, I argued that if a president does anything illegal, unlawful, or criminal-like—if he commits treason, bribery or other high crimes and misdemeanors – the criteria for impeachment under the Constitution are met. But if a president engages in entirely lawful conduct motivated in part by the desire to be reelected, which he believes is in the public interest, that would not constitute grounds for impeachment. Everybody seemed to understand the distinction I was drawing. Some agreed, others disagreed. But the distinction was clear between illegal conduct on the one hand, and lawful conduct on the other hand.

Two days later I returned to the Senate to answer questions put to the lawyers by the senators. The first question to me came from Senator Ted Cruz. He asked whether a *quid pro quo* constituted an impeachable offense. My response was consistent with my argument two days earlier: I said that what "would make a *quid pro quo* unlawful is if the *quo* were in some way *illegal*." If it were, it could constitute an impeachable offense. But if it wasn't illegal or unlawful, the president's political motives could not turn it into an impeachable offense. That was quite clear. Indeed, the next question from the senators was directed to the Democratic House Manager, who was asked to respond to my answer. Congressman Adam Schiff disagreed with my answer, but understood the distinction between lawful and unlawful. So did CNN. When they first showed my answer, they showed it in full, including my statement that a *quid pro quo* would not be impeachable so long as it was not "in some way illegal." I then went on to say that if a president was motivated in part by his desire to be reelected, which he believe was in the public interest, that motive would not turn a lawful act into an impeachable offense.

But then CNN made a decision to doctor and edit my recorded remarks so as to eliminate all references to "unlawful" or "illegal" conduct. They wanted their viewers to believe that I had told the Senate that a president could do anything—even commit such crimes as "bribery" and "extortion"—as long as he was motivated by a desire to be reelected. That, of course, was precisely the opposite of what I said. And that is precisely the reason why CNN edited and doctored the tape the way they did: namely, to deliberately create the false impression that I had said the president could commit any crimes in order to be reelected, without fear of impeachment.

CNN then got its paid commentators to go on the air, show the doctored recording and rail against me for saying that a president could commit crimes with impunity. Joe Lockhart, former White House Press Secretary under President Clinton, said that I had given the president "license to commit crimes" and that: "This is what you hear from Stalin. This is what you hear from Mussolini, what you hear from authoritarians, from Hitler, from all the authoritarian people who rationalize, in some cases genocide, based what was in the public interest."

No one corrected him by pointing out that I said exactly the opposite in the sentence that CNN had edited out. Nor did anyone correct Paul Begala when he wrote, "The Dershowitz Doctrine would make presidents immune from *every criminal act*, so long as they could plausibly claim they did it to boost their re-election effort. Campaign finance laws: out the window. *Bribery* statutes: gone. *Extortion*: no more. This is Donald Trump's fondest figurative dream: to be able to shoot someone on Fifth Avenue and get away with it."

CNN is, of course, responsible for the decision to edit and doctor the recording to reverse its meaning and they are also responsible for how their paid commentators mis-characterized what I said.

So I am suing them for a lot of money, not in order to enrich myself, but to deter CNN and other media from maliciously misinforming their viewers at the expense of innocent people. I intend to donate funds I receive from CNN to worthy charities, including those that defend the First Amendment. Every American will benefit from a judicial decision that holds giant media accountable for turning truth on its head and for placing partisanship above the public interest. So I will continue to defend the First Amendment as I have for the last fifty-five years (I am now consulting with Julian Assange's legal team). But I will insist that giant media not abuse their First Amendment rights in the way that CNN did.

F. The Constitutional Case Against the Senate Trying Citizen Trump

[After President Trump was impeached by the House, I wrote a series of articles pointing to the dangers this posed to civil liberties.]

Once President Trump leaves office on January 20, and becomes a private citizen, the Senate loses jurisdiction to try him on impeachment. The text of the Constitution seems clear: "the president ... shall be removed from office on impeachment ... and conviction." Thus, the purpose and function of House impeachment and Senate trial and conviction is removal from office. If a sitting President is impeached and convicted, he can *ALSO* be disqualified from holding future office, but that is an *additional* punishment to removal, not an alternative to removal. The Constitution mandates that "Judgment in cases of impeachment shall not extend further than to removal, *and* disqualification..." (emphasis added) The Constitution deliberately used the word "and," which is the conjunctive, rather than "or," which would be the disjunctive. The Senate has no authority to disqualify anyone who has not been removed. It has no jurisdiction to try an ordinary citizen— even an ex-president.

It doesn't matter that President Trump was impeached by the House while still serving. It wouldn't even matter if the Senate began its *trial* while he was still in office. The Senate loses jurisdiction over him as soon as his term ends and he is no longer subject to removal. This seems clear, not only from the text of the impeachment provisions of the Constitution, but also from the intention of the Framers. James Madison, the father of our Constitution, clearly stated that "the President of the United States is impeachable *at any time during his continuance in office.*" (emphasis added) At the time of the Framing, several states did allow impeachment of public officials after they left office. Members of the Constitutional Convention, some of whom represented these states, were aware of this process and they could easily have included it in our Constitution. But they chose not to. They also chose explicitly to prohibit the British practice of having the legislature try and punish specific individuals. The framers included a specific prohibition against Congress passing any "bill of attainder," which is any legislative act punishing a specifically named individual. The courts have ruled that the punishments prohibited by the Bill of Attainder clause include disqualification from holding office. The only exception to the prohibition against trial by legislature is a Senate trial to remove an impeached office holder. These is no exception for merely disqualifying a former or possibly future officeholder. Moreover, the constitution requires the Chief Justice to preside "when the President of the United is tried," not when the former or possibly future President is tried as a private citizen. The Senate has no power to try or to punish Donald Trump once his presidency has ended.

There is one case, back in 1876, of a cabinet member being tried by the Senate after he resigned his office, but it is a controversial precedent that is not binding on the current Senate and whether it can place a former President on trial. Secretary of War William W. Belknap was indisputably guilty of numerous impeachable offences, to which he confessed and resigned his office. Nevertheless, the House unanimously impeached him and, despite his resignation,

37 to 29 that it had the power to try him.
thirds) were needed to convict him. The
35 to 25 for conviction—five votes short.
of the votes for acquittal were cast by senators who believed he was guilty but that the Senate lacked
jurisdiction to try a former cabinet member who had
already left office. The nature of the votes, therefore, does
not make this a compelling precedent for trying a former
President after his term has ended. No former President or
former high ranking officer has even been convicted by the
senate of an impeachable offense.

A far more relevant precedent would be the decision
by Congress *not* to impeach and try Richard Nixon after
he resigned. When Nixon resigned to avoid facing certain
impeachment and conviction, there was no movement
to continue the impeachment process after he left office.
This, despite the fact that Nixon committed indisputably impeachable offences and that there was widespread
bi-partisan support and enough votes for his removal. But
wiser heads prevailed, and no effort was made to pile on
by impeaching and trying him after he left office. I am sure
that at least part of the reason was the grave doubt that
Congress had jurisdiction to put a private citizen, albeit
an ex-president, on trial. Another negative precedent
involved Aaron Burr, who planned an insurrection. Some

of the planning may have begun while he was still serving as Vice President, but it was not revealed until after he left office. It never occurred to members of the framing generation to *impeach* Burr. Instead, he was *prosecuted* for his alleged offense—and acquitted.

Beyond the constitutional prohibition against trying a former president in the Senate, there are strong policy and historical reasons against an incoming administration taking recriminations against a former president who lost reelection. Unlike other countries, where defeated former presidents are routinely prosecuted, our nation has lived more in accordance with President Lincoln's message to the soon-to-be-defeated Confederacy: "With Malice toward none, with **charity for** all, with **firmness in the right**, as **God gives us to see the right**, let us strive on to finish the work we are in, to bind up the nation's wounds."

It would set a terrible precedent for the victorious Democrats to recriminate against the defeated former president.

Moreover, it would distract from president Biden's agenda and his express goal of healing our divided nation.

So the case against putting Citizen Trump on trial in the Senate after he leaves office is far more compelling than the case for putting him on trial.

G. The House Managers' Brief Endangers our Freedom of Speech

[When the House Managers filed their brief, I published the following op-ed.]

The brief filed by the House managers advocating the conviction and disqualification of citizen Donald trump contains a frontal attack on freedom of speech for all Americans. It states categorically that "the first amendment does not apply *at all* to impeachment proceedings," despite the express language of that amendment prohibiting "Congress" from making any law, or presumably taking any other action, that abridges "the freedom of speech."

The brief is based on a flawed reading of history and on a misunderstanding of the role of freedom of speech in governance.

Its discussion of "free speech" begins with a sentence that reveals its fundamental error: "The First Amendment exists to promote our democratic system." This categorical statement would surely have surprised the Framers of the First Amendment, who believed in freedom of speech, but not so much in democracy. The Framers of our constitutional system thought they were building a "republic," with limited suffrage and many checks on "democracy."

The electoral college, as conceived by the Framers, was anything but democratic. State legislatures could select the electors without even allowing eligible voters to participate in the process. Moreover, only a small fraction of citizens and residents were eligible to vote: white, male, 21-year-old, landowners—and even those were subject to varying disqualifications. The Senate was selected by state legislatures, not democratic voting.

"It's a republic, if you can keep it," proclaimed Benjamin Franklin. Freedom of speech was essential to keeping it a republic, not necessarily a democracy.

Over the years, we have evolved into a democracy, with near-universal suffrage, direct election of senators, and voting for presidential electors, but we would still be guaranteed the protections of the First Amendment even if we had not adopted these attributes of democracy. So, no, the First Amendment does not exist only to "protect our democratic system." It exists to protect our liberty, regardless of what system we choose. If Americans were to vote to restore the British monarchy, as some Tories advocated both before and after the American revolution, the First Amendment would still guarantee us the right to dissent. The First Amendment is not merely a means to securing a particular form of government; the freedom of speech it guarantees is an end unto itself—an independent good, under any system of governance.

Why is this historic point so important? Because the argument made by the House Managers—that the First Amendment doesn't apply to presidents or others who

"attack our democracy"—was precisely the argument made
by Joseph McCarthy and his followers when they sought to
deny First Amendment protection to communists and others
who were seen as enemies of democracy who, if they came
to power, would deny the rest of us our freedoms, including
of free speech. Those of us who fought against McCarthyism
understood, better than the House Managers, that freedom
of speech must include those who would replace democracy
with other systems of governance. It must even include those
who advocate severe restrictions on freedom of speech, as
many young left-wing radicals do today. They, too, must be
allowed to express their dangerous views.

The brief goes on to argue that even if the First
Amendment were deemed applicable to impeachment, "A First Amendment defense would still fail,"
because President Trump's speech "plainly satisfies" the
Brandenburg principle. That is simply wrong as a matter
of constitutional law. President Trump's speech is clearly
within the protection of Brandenburg. He did not "incite"
violence. To the contrary, he called for a peaceful and patriotic protest. Moreover, he advocated, rather than incited.
The difference is clear. An incitement is a directive to a
crowd to act immediately and lawlessly. Trump's speech was
made a mile away from the capitol, and although he used
strong words, these words are typical of calls to action that
have been held to be protected by the First Amendment.

Hundreds of speakers, some of whom I and the ACLU have represented, have made similar harangues that fell within Constitutional protections. Indeed, even the ACLU, which supported Trump's second impeachment, seemed to have implicitly acknowledged that his speech may fall within the protections of Brandenburg. They now appear to have changed their position, arguing that "Trump's speech was not protected by Brandenberg."

Perhaps the most fundamental flaw in the House Manager's brief is that they regard impeachment as "fundamentally an employment action against a public official." They make the following absurd argument: "Thus, just as a president may legitimately demand the resignation of a cabinet secretary who publicly disagrees with him on a matter of policy . . . the public's elected representatives may disqualify the president from federal office when they recognize that his public statements constitute a violation of his oath of office and a high crime against the constitutional order." But the analogy between a president firing a cabinet secretary and Congress removing and disqualifying a president flies in the face of the Constitution. The Framers explicitly rejected the British parliamentary system, in which "the public's elected representatives" may remove a prime minister by a simple majority vote of no confidence. Instead, they imposed rigid criteria for removing and disqualifying a president – criteria that requires proof of treason, bribery, and other high crimes and misdemeanors. Impeachment and removal is not "fundamentally an employment action." It is a grave interference with democracy that can result in a small number of elected officials removing a duly elected president and denying the public's right to vote for him or her in a future election. To fail to understand that distinction is to fail to understand the Constitution.

H. Is the University of Chicago Requiring Loyalty Oaths from Its Faculty?

[Restrictions on freedom of expression by universities are not limited to those who supported Trump. In this article, I discuss "loyalty oaths"]

The University of Chicago's English department, which has been ranked nationally as top in its field, has declared a set of beliefs to which its faculty is "committing." Its announcement began with the following *mea culpa*: "English as a discipline" has encouraged "colonization, exploitation, extraction and anti-Blackness." It then expressed the faculty's collective belief: "In light of this historical reality, we believe that undoing persistent, recalcitrant anti-Blackness in our discipline and in our institutions must be the collective responsibility of all faculty, here and elsewhere." Finally, it announced that "for the 2020-2021 graduate admissions cycle" it will accept "only applicants interested in working in and with Black

Studies." It is this last restriction that has generated the most interest—and criticism. But it is the formal declaration of a collective creed by a university department that is most troubling.

Any individual faculty member is entitled to commit him or herself to what the English Department calls "the struggle of Black and Indigenous people and all racialized and dispossessed people, against inequality and brutality," but no department has the right to compel its faculty, staff or students to subscribe to any set of beliefs or commit to any "struggle." Universities, and departments within universities, must be open to all points of view, beliefs and struggles. In totalitarian countries around the world, universities are required to be aligned with governmentally approved values. And when I was in college, some universities required teachers to take loyalty oaths against Communism.

But in the United States today, professors and students must remain free to come to their own conclusions, to arrive at their own beliefs and to decide for themselves which struggles are most important. That is what real diversity requires: not only diversity of race and ethnicity, but diversity of thought, belief, and commitment, not imposed uniformity.

What if a faculty member or student does not "believe" that studying Shakespeare, Melville, Faulkner, Lewis Carroll, Virginia Woolf, George Orwell and Alice Walker has actually encouraged these evils? Will such faculty members or students be evaluated fairly and their work judged objectively?

How would the University of Chicago English department deal with a Zionist scholar who strongly believes that the struggle against anti-Semitism and anti-Zionism is as important as the struggle of "dispossessed people?"

Would it allow University of Pennsylvania professor Adolph Reed, an African American Marxist, to argue, as he does, that race—i.e., Blackness—is less important than class, in struggling against an unjust society?

Would it allow professors to assign Martin Luther King's speech in which the civil rights leader dreams of living in a nation where people will "not be judged by the color of their skin, but by the content of their character?" Will it disqualify any professor who is opposed to identity politics or race-based affirmative action?

Allowing a university department to impose its collective beliefs on all professors and students is a core violation of academic freedom. It threatens freedom of speech and conscience. It coerces compliance by dissidents who fear cancellation and discrimination. It risks turning great universities into propaganda mills for political correctness. Most frighteningly, it threatens to produce a generation of leaders who have not been taught how to think for themselves, but instead have been indoctrinated into a groupthink reminiscent of Orwell's *1984*—a book which I doubt will ever be assigned by the University of Chicago's brave new English curriculum.

Nor does the Chicago English department want to limit its imposed beliefs only to its own faculty and students. It insists that "all faculty, here and elsewhere" commit to its "struggle" and follow its lead. I hope they don't. It's the road to conformity and tyranny of the mind, even if well intentioned.

House Managers: Good Politics, Bad Constitutional Law

The House Managers spent the first full day of trial laying out the timeline that led to the attack on the capitol. They showed videos, tweets, and other documents. It made for good theater and good politics, but very bad constitutional law.

Several of the Managers focused on Trump's repeated claims from the night of the election until the day he left office that the election was stolen, fraudulent and unfair—and that *he* really won the election. The managers intended this to help their constitutional case, but it hurt it. Proving that Trump's statements were false *does not* in any way strengthen their argument that they were not fully protected by the First Amendment. The Supreme

Court has held over and over again that the Constitution does not distinguish between true and false statements. A false claim that the earth is flat is as constitutionally protected as conclusive evidence that the earth is round. A mendacious canard that the Holocaust did not occur is as protected as the fact that six million Jews were murdered. And President Trump's statement, false as it may be, that the election was stolen is as constitutionally protected as the true claim that President Biden was legitimately elected. And Trump's opinion, even if based on nothing more than wishful thinking, is protected by the Constitution.

Moreover, the Supreme Court has also held that there is no such thing as a *false* opinion under the First Amendment. Jamie Raskin, who is my former student, and then a professor of constitutional law, understands this. Why, then, is he spending so much time on establishing that Trump made false claims about the election? There are two possible explanations: the first is that this is political theater and the videos are very effective in undercutting Trump's credibility. If this is the explanation, then this trial is more about persuading future voters than current Senators. The second explanation may be that the House Managers are trying to lay a trap for the Trump legal team. By focusing so heavily on Trump's election claims, they may be hoping to force the Trump lawyers to defend Trump's views on the election. If the Trump lawyers fall into this trap, they will be making a serious blunder. If the Senate trial turns into a debate as to whether or not President Biden was duly and fairly elected, Trump will lose several Senators who believe that he did not commit an impeachable offense, but who also believe that the election was not stolen.

One reason why I decided not to appear as counsel in this case is precisely because I was afraid I might be drawn into a discussion of the validity of the election. I personal believe the election was generally fair and I could not credibly argue the opposite. I suspect that Trump's lawyers may feel the same discomfort, but they are not free to express their personal views if directed not to do so by their client. I, however, am completely free to defend President Trump's speeches in the court of public opinion on the grounds of constitutional law alone.

One Democratic senator had the temerity to ask the Trump lawyers whether they *personally* believed the election was stolen. It was an utterly improper question to ask a lawyer, and he properly declined to answer.

Another ploy used by the Managers is to constantly to refer to President Trump as "our Commander in Chief" or "the Commander in Chief." Not only is this a false characterization of the constitutional role of the president, it is extraordinarily dangerous. The United States has no

Commander in Chief. No president can tell us what to do. Every American has the right to refuse to comply with any order of a president—except, of course a member of the armed forces. Under our Constitution, the President is not the Commander in Chief of the nation. He is only the Commander in Chief of the Armed Forces. In totalitarian countries, the president is the commander in chief of the people. Dictators wear military uniforms and tell their citizen what to do and not to do. Presidents are civilians, and they have no authority to command obedience from other civilians.

The House Managers made this totalitarian argument in order to mislead Senators and viewers into believing that the people who trashed the Capitol were acting under orders from the President. Nothing could be further from the truth. First of all, only *some* who listened to the President's speech went to the capitol. Many dispersed and when home. Only *some* who went to the capitol broke in and committed violence. If any of them thought they were obliged to follow the president's orders, it is precisely because the media misled them into thinking that was the case.

So let's be clear, all of the President's statements quoted by the House Managers, from the night of the election to the day he left office, were constitutionally protected. Not a single one of them violated the *Brandenburg* criteria for incitement. Nor was he the Commander in Chief of the people ,who committed crimes in the Capitol. They were individual citizens, who bear responsibility for their own crimes.

So my former student Jamie Raskin may deserve a Tony for producing a good show. But he gets a B- from his former teacher for constructing a constitutional argument.

How the First Amendment Saved Jamie Raskin's Father

I like Congressman Jamie Raskin. He was my former student, a distinguished professor of constitutional law, and now a progressive member of congress leading the House Managers in their effort to have the Senate convict and disqualify former President Trump.

During one of his Senate speeches, he quoted his late, great father, Marcus Raskin, whom I also knew. I met Marcus, a prominent left wing intellectual, when he was indicted for conspiracy to obstruct the Vietnam war effort by encouraging young men to resist the draft. He coauthored a call to resist illegitimate authority, and stood trial along with doctor Benjamin Spock and others who advocated the burning of draft cards, brea- ins at draft boards, and other unlawful actions to obstruct the war effort. Many young people did what was advocated and were punished for their unlawful acts.

Marcus, who was charged only with inciting these unlawful acts by others, was represented by my mentor, teacher, and dear friend General Telford Taylor, who had been America's chief prosecutor at the Nuremberg trials. I consulted with Taylor on Marcus's defense, which ultimately prevailed.

Not surprisingly, an important part of the defense was that the First Amendment protected Marcus's advocacy of resistance to the draft, even if such resistance took the form of unlawful actions by others. Civil libertarians and liberals from all across the country rallied to the defense of "the Spock 5," invoking the First Amendment.

The jury acquitted Marcus, and the Court of Appeals reversed the convictions of the other defendants. They were all saved by a broad reading of the First Amendment.

Several years later, Marcus was once again protected by a broad reading of the First Amendment when he served as an intermediary between Daniel Ellsberg, who unlawfully stole the Pentagon Papers, and *The New York Times*, which published them despite their being classified. But for the First Amendment, Marcus would have been charged with conspiracy to publish classified material.

Now, Marcus' son Jamie is quoting his father in a speech that would cut the heart out of the very First Amendment that twice saved his father. Had he not quoted his heroic father, I would not be focusing on the different views expressed by father and son, but by invoking his father, Jamie invited the comparison. If Jamie Raskin's current view of the First Amendment had prevailed back in the day, his father would likely have been convicted of two felonies. If President Trump incited his followers to commit unlawful conduct , so did Marcus. I believe that neither incited and that both were protected by the First Amendment.

Fortunately for his father and for all liberty-loving Americans, Jamie's current views were soundly rejected during the golden age of freedom of speech. That golden age has now been tarnished beyond recognition by Jamie Raskin's narrow, partisan misreading of the First Amendment.

Nor is he alone. Hundreds of members of Congress, academics, and ordinary Americans seem willing to compromise our fundamental freedoms of speech, expression, and assembly in order to create a "Trump exception" to the First Amendment.

I would have thought that Jamie Raskin—in light of his history as a constitutional law professor, his family history under the First Amendment, and his own protests against the 2016 election—would be leading the charge to protect the First Amendment. But no! He is leading the charge to compromise then-President Trump's free speech rights, and thus the rights of all Americans to express controversial, even wrongheaded and provocative, views.

Jamie Raskin has tried to distinguish his father's invocation of the First Amendment from Donald Trump's on the ground that his father was an ordinary citizen protesting the actions of the government, whereas President Trump was the government. But the First Amendment recognizes no such distinction. Moreover, President Trump was protesting the actions of other branches of government—wrongly, in my view, but constitutionally nonetheless.

Marcus Raskin's broad invocation of the First Amendment to protect his advocacy of unlawful acts of protest sets the correct standard under which such speech should be judged. Jamie Raskin's far narrower and more partisan view of the First Amendment is inconsistent with that standard. I hope that the next time Jamie Raskin quotes his wonderful father, he will remind his listeners how the same First Amendment that he is seeking to narrow protected his father's just and righteous protests against the Vietnam War, as well his own unrighteous protests against the 2016 election.

Free speech for me and my father, but not for Donald Trump, is not the American way.

When Liberals Demand Social Media Censorship, Free Speech Is Really In Trouble

Common Cause has always presented itself as a centrist, sensible liberal organization, advocating evolution, not revolution. Its leaders cross party lines and advocate democratic principles, which have traditionally included the open marketplace of ideas. It proudly proclaims its commitment to "empowering voices to be heard."

The organization distinguishes itself from the radical left, which has a history of advocating free speech for me but not for thee—free speech for the left but censorship for the right. Not so, Common Cause. Until now, it has advocated free speech for all as an important part of democratic governance.

The culture of free speech— "empowering voices to be heard"— transcends the First Amendment, which is applicable only to state action: that is, action taken by governmental entities. The culture of free speech, however, extends to private institutions as well, such as non-public universities, large corporations, and the increasingly influential social media. Now, Common Cause has broken with its past defense of free speech culture and has demanded that Facebook, and presumably other platforms, censor Donald Trump and possibly his followers, supporters and enablers. Here is what they have said:

"Trump cannot be allowed back on Facebook.

Donald Trump abused his wide reach on social media for months to spread baseless—and as we saw on January 6th, dangerous—lies about our election.

He repeatedly violated Facebook's civic integrity rules and jeopardized our entire democracy. But as of now, Facebook has only 'indefinitely suspended' Trump's account—and they may be on the cusp of letting him back onto the platform.

We can't let Facebook give Trump another opportunity to mislead voters and stroke chaos on its website.

Sign the Petition: Tell Facebook to permanently ban Donald Trump

Now, Facebook has created a new Oversight Board that will review its decision to ban Trump—and the most impactful thing that this board can do is decide to make that ban permanent.

The team at Facebook urgently needs to hear from consumers like you and me. I hope you'll speak out today.

Thanks for all you do.

Common Cause Team

Common Cause, of course, is entitled to its views under the First Amendment. So, too, is the social media. They can pick and choose whomever they want to post, censor, edit, or warn about. That is their legal right. But critics of private censorship have the right to condemn them for choosing the way they censor the marketplace of ideas.

I am one such critic. I defend the legal right of Common Cause to demand censorship by the social media, and I defend the right of the social media to engage in selective censorship, but I reserve my own moral and political right to condemn both Common Cause and social media for depriving citizens of the right to hear even outrageous and wrong-headed views. I trust our citizens to use their own common sense in deciding what to believe or disbelieve, while fully understanding the dangers of circulating false information. The Big Lie sometimes gets believed. But what is worse than the Big Lie being believed is the censor denying us the right to decide what to believe or disbelieve.

I am shocked that Common Cause, which is devoted to the pursuit of democratic principles, is so frightened of the open marketplace of ideas that it feels the need to demand that some ideas not be made available on social media.

Nor is Common Cause alone among liberals in calling for selective censorship against Trump and his supporters. Nicholas Kristof of *The New York Times* has called on advertisers to boycott Fox and other media that support Trump and his "fellow travelers" (remember that term from McCarthyism?) "at Fox, OANN and Newsmax." He has also called on "cable companies to drop Fox News from basic cable TV packages." Two members of Congress have

followed Kristof's lead, urging cable and satellite companies no longer to carry these conservative channels.

This is right out of the Joe McCarthy playbook, with its
"red channels" and "Hollywood blacklist." And this from
a liberal who claims to be opposed to "cancel culture" and
"liberal intolerance." His own liberal tolerance seems to
end with Fox and Newsmax, which he distinguishes from
CNN and Rachel Maddow, which he says merely "make
mistakes," but don't deliberately spin "nonsense into rat-
ings gold!" Why not let the market place decide what is
nonsense? We don't need private or public censors, liberals
or conservatives, telling us what to believe.

A Victory for the Constitution, Not So Much for Trump

The Senate decision vote to acquit former President Trump
by a vote of 57 to 43 (a two thirds majority was need to convict), was a modest victory for the Constitution. Whether
the 43 Senators voted to acquit on the ground that the
Senate has no jurisdiction over a private citizen, or on the
ground that Trump's speech was protected by the First
Amendment, the Constitution was vindicated. Senate
minority leader Mitch McConnell, in a scathing attack on
Trump, explained that his vote to acquit was based, in large
part, on the fact that the former president was now a private citizen. He correctly observed that the Senate does

not have a roving commission to impeach and disqualify former office holders. To conclude otherwise would be to empower Congress to disempower tens of millions of voters from casting ballots for their candidates of choice.

President Trump is now free to run for election in 2024. The Senate's decision to acquit Trump also supports the First Amendment, which was intended to protect the kind of controversial, even dangerous, speech that President Trump delivered on January 6th. To have ruled otherwise would have disemboweled the First Amendment in the context of presidential rhetoric about elections. I agree with Senator McConnell that Trump was wrong in arguing that the election was stolen and fraudulent, but the First Amendment protects wrong opinions as surely as it does correct ones. President Trump had as much right to say erroneously that the election was unfair as President Biden the right to say correctly that he was elected fairly. And we have the right to judge each of them and their allegations morally and politically, but not legally.

If Trump were to run against Biden in 2024, all Americans can vote based in part on who they think was telling the truth about the 2020 election.

Although the Senate vote allows citizen Trump to run for election again in 2024, the trial itself has made it less likely that he will be able to do so successfully. The Democratic House Managers presented a devastating picture of the events at the Capitol and of Trump's moral and political responsibility for creating an atmosphere that may well have contributed to the violence. McConnell's speech agreed with much of that case. But there is an enormous difference between moral and political responsibility on the one hand and constitutional liability under the First Amendment on the other hand. But it is the former that may well determine Trump's political fate.

The speech he gave on January 6, though constitutionally protected, was irresponsible, especially in light of the rhetoric that proceeded it for several months. In my view, and in the view of many thoughtful Americans of both parties, including Senator McConnell, the election was not stolen. There may well have been mistakes, both of a legal and factual nature. But these mistakes are unlikely to have produced enough of a disparity to change the outcome. Biden, after all, decisively won both the electoral college and popular vote. There is a heavy burden of proof on those challenging the outcome of an election, and based on the evidence I have seen, that burden was not satisfied by Trump and his lawyers. Moreover, there are processes for challenging flawed elections. These processes include internal reviews within state election institutions, as well as judicial review by the courts. Although I think it would have been better if the courts had conducted more extensive reviews on the merits and demerits of the claims, the processes went forward lawfully and fairly.

Trump was wrong, in my view, not to concede after it became clear that he had exhausted all appropriate remedies, and he was wrong not to attend the Biden inauguration. He was also wrong to call on protesters to descend on the Capitol on the day they were certifying the electoral college votes. He had the constitutional right to say what he said, but he was wrong, in my view and that of Senator McConnell and others, to exercise that right in the manner he did.

History will judge Trump harshly for his conduct between November 6 and January 20. But history will also harshly judge the Democrats and Republicans who organized and voted for the impeachments of President Trump for conduct that does not come within the constitutional criteria authorizing impeachment.

This op-ed will anger both opponents and supporters of Trump. But it should please all those who place allegiance to the Constitution above allegiance to person or party.

Falsely Charging McConnell with Inconsistency

CNN and other left-wing media went on rampages after Senator Mitch McConnell delivered his speech explaining why he voted to acquit Donald Trump, despite his belief that Trump had engaged in improper behavior. They accused McConnell of hypocrisy and inconsistency, arguing that if he believed Trump had done wrong, he was obligated to vote for conviction. But it is CNN and the other media who failed to understand the distinction between defending the Constitution and defending the person.

McConnell taught the American people a civics lesson by explaining that the Senate had no constitutional authority to place a former president on trial, even one who had been impeached while still serving in office. In doing so, he echoed a constitutional argument I have been making from the very beginning of this unconstitutional power grab by the Democratic-controlled Congress. The language of the constitution is clear that "The President ... shall be removed from office on impeachment for, and conviction of, treason and bribery and other crimes and misdemeanors." The constitutional power to impeach and remove does not extend beyond federal civil officials who are still in office and can be removed. As James Madison, the father of our Constitution, wrote in Federalist 39: "The president of the United States is impeachable at any time during his continuation in office." It is true that once removed, they can also be disqualified, but they cannot be disqualified unless they are first removed. The Senate voted by a majority that they had power that the Constitution denied them, but McConnell dissented from that vote, along with numerous other Senators, and they acted on their dissenting views in voting to acquit. They were right to do so. That is precisely what happened in the *Belknap* case, which was cited by the House Managers as a precedent.

The House Managers argued in their brief that the power to impeach is *not* limited to *officials* who remain in office, but can extend back to any person who held federal office, despite how many years ago that person left the office. To have voted to convict citizen Trump would have given Congress a roving commission to seek out and disqualify any potential candidate who had ever held federal public office. McConnell correctly rejected that open-ended power grab.

The most important lesson taught by McConnell is that the Constitution protects both the good and the bad, the agreeable and the disagreeable, Republicans and Democrats. One does not have to agree with the substance of what President Trump did or said on January 6 in order to correctly conclude that the Senate had no jurisdiction over him once he left office, and that the statements he made—whatever one might think of them—are fully protected by the Constitution.

Back in the bad old days of McCarthyism, anyone who supported the constitutional rights of accused Communists was deemed to support Communism. That was wrong then, just as it is wrong today to believe that everyone who defends Trump against an unconstitutional impeachment necessarily supports his views or actions. I, for one, have been quite critical of Trump's actions on January 6, but strongly defend his right to have made the speech, even though I think he was wrong to do so. I also defend his right not to be placed on trial as a private citizen by the Senate.

So three cheers for Mitch McConnell for trying to educate the American public about this important distinction. No cheers for CNN and other left wing media for returning us to the days of McCarthyism, when these distinctions were deliberately blurred.

The End of the Trump Era—At Least For Now

The acquittal of Donald Trump on charges of inciting an insurrection marks the end of the current Trump era. From its very beginning during the runup to the 2016 election, Trump exacerbated the already-palpable divisions within our nation. Trump's campaign for president was marked by name calling, personal attacks, and exaggerated claims. He won the election fair and square, as I predicted he would in August of 2016. I did not support his candidacy, having campaigned for, contributed to, and voted for Hillary Clinton. But I accepted the outcome of the election, despite inexcusable actions by then-FBI director James Comey in accusing Hillary Clinton of improper conduct with regard to her emails.

The Trump presidency was filled with controversy, ranging from his ban on immigration from designated Muslim countries, to his policies on the Mexican border, to his inconsistencies with regard to COVID-19, and finally to his unwillingness to accept the outcome of the 2020 election.

The Trump era ends with even more division than existed when it began. Trump contributed to that, but so did his enemies. Trump haters demanded that everyone choose sides and pass purity tests. I failed both, refusing to give up my right to assess his presidency in a nuanced fashion. I opposed many of his policies, but I strongly supported his approach to the Middle East peace process. Not only did I support President Trump on the Middle East, I actively helped his administration in their efforts to achieve peace between Israel and the Palestinians and normalcy between Israel and its Sunni Arab neighbors. Having opposed President Obama's ill-advised Iran deal, I supported Trump's tougher approach to the Mullah's nuclear ambitions. I supported the movement of the U.S. embassy from Tel Aviv to Jerusalem: I had unsuccessfully urged several previous presidents to make that move. I also supported the Trump administration's recognition of Israel's annexation of the Golan Heights, subject to negotiation with Syria in any future peace deal.

Among the most serious and potentially enduring constitutional casualties of the Trump/anti-Trump era were
freedoms of speech, the press, and assembly. The First
Amendment is weaker today than it was when Trump took
office. This is largely the fault of anti-Trump zealots, though
Trump himself provoked the overreaction by the manner in
which he exercised his freedom of expression. His Tweets
and other social media statements caused several platforms
to ban him and others with whose speech they disagreed.
Trump's excesses provoked traditionally liberal organizations such as Common Cause and liberal writers such as
Nicholas Kristof to call for private censorship and to emu-
late some of the tactics that had long been condemned by
liberals as McCarthyism. Trump's second impeachment,
based on a speech that most civil libertarians would have
found to be protected by the First Amendment had it been
delivered by anyone else, damaged the First Amendment,
despite his ultimate acquittal.

Another casualty of the Trump era was the judicial
selection process, especially with regard to the Supreme
Court. Trump's first two nominations were reasonable,
though as a liberal they would not have been my choices.
Senator Schumer's angry threats against them were
unreasonable. The manner by which Justice Kavanaugh
was treated by Democrats and liberals was nothing short
of disgraceful, but he was eventually confirmed, largely

along party lines. It was Trump's final nomination of Amy Coney Barrett that exposed the hypocrisy of Republican Senate leaders, who had opposed President Obama's nomination of Merrick Garland eight months before the election, on the ground that the next president should make that appointment. But when President Trump nominated Barrett, much closer to the 2020 election, the same Republican senators rushed it through to confirmation, coming up with phony distinctions. Now, there is a move to pack the court with Democratic appointees, and President Biden has appointed a commission to look into the entire process of judicial appointments.

From a civil-liberties perspective, we are worse off today than we were four years ago. The blame for this is shared. Trump provoked his enemies into overreaction against our civil liberties. Those who supported his impeachment tried to create a "Trump exception" to the First Amendment, as a reaction to the "January exception" that they feared would be created by not impeaching him for his January 6 incendiary speech.

The time has come not only to reunite Americans, to rebuild shattered friendships, and to move forward with malice toward none and charity for all. The time has also come to re-strengthen our civil liberties, most especially our First Amendment rights. Now that Trump is no longer president, I hope that fair-weather civil libertarians who were willing to compromise our rights in the interests of "getting Trump" will come to their senses and understand that our constitutional rights are more important than any president and must endure beyond any presidency.

Don't Confuse The Left With Liberalism

Many on the right blame "liberals" for the current spate of censorship and cancel culture. In doing so, they confuse liberals with leftists. There is a critical distinction.

Liberals are tolerant and open-minded. We welcome debate on divisive issues. We are even sometimes persuaded to change our minds. We try to disagree without being disagreeable. We do not end friendships over political disagreements. We do not impose our values and preferences on others. We accept George Bernard Shaw's admonition: "*Do not do unto others as you would that they should do unto you. Their tastes may not be the same.*"

We defend the civil liberties of everyone, even those who would deny our liberties. We demand due process, freedom of expression, and the right to assemble for all, even those we abhor. We are process-oriented— fair elections, fair trials — rather than result-oriented. We understand that fair processes will sometimes produce bad results, but that is the price we pay for democracy.

The above characteristics do not describe many on today's left. Especially since the election of Donald Trump, many on the left have abandoned tolerance, open-mind-edness, civil discourse, free speech, and due process. They have devised a "Trump exception" to civil liberties. They insist that Trump is different: that his presidency posed unique dangers to democratic values. They have short memories. History shows that in nearly every generation, result-oriented and intolerant extremists have found excuses to deny civil liberties to their enemies.

A few examples will suffice to prove my point: In the earliest days of our democracy, George Washington supported the Alien and Sedition laws put forward by the Adams administration, which denied free speech to Jeffersonians. Abraham Lincoln suspended the writ of *habeas corpus* during the civil war. Woodrow Wilson autho-rized the Palmer Raids and closed our borders to Jews and other "undesirables." Franklin Delano Roosevelt detained more than 100,000 Americans of Japanese descent. Senator McCarthy denied due process to accused Communists and their enablers. All of these were done in the name of "emergencies." "This is different," opponents of civil liber-ties would argue.

Now it is the left that is insisting that Trump was dif-ferent and that his words and deeds justified constraining constitutional rights, especially free speech and due pro-cess. It is many on the left who have been intolerant of opposing views, who have ended long-time friendships with those with whom they disagree, who would report lawyers to bar associations, and who would keep Trump supporters off university campuses.

Traditionally, many on the center left have also been liberals and civil libertarians. That has never been true of the hard left, which has always been intolerant of free speech and due process for those with whom they disagree. The Trump years moved many from the center left to the hard left, especially with regard to civil liberties. That is a great tragedy. There used to be a large number of civil libertarians on the center left who exhibited the characteristics of liberalism described above. The Trump presidency truncated that group to near oblivion. Under Trump, everyone had to choose sides. Tolerance became a vice, not a virtue. Free Speech and censorship became weapons to be used selectively in favor of one side and against the other. Free speech for me, but not for thee became free speech for those who opposed Trump, but not for those who supported him.

Those of us who opposed Trump's policies but supported his constitutional rights found ourselves isolated and lonely. We were attacked by the left for supporting Trump's constitutional rights, and we were attacked by the right for not supporting Trump's policies. I felt comfortable in my principled isolation, but my family paid a heavy price for my insistence on remaining a liberal civil libertarian rather than choosing partisan sides.

Now that Trump is no longer president, I can only hope that some of those erstwhile liberals who were pushed to the intolerant left by the perceived "emergency" and danger presented by Trump will now return to the liberal center and appreciate the virtues of free speech and due process for all. If a "Trump exception" to civil liberties were to be accepted, it would soon be applied to other perceived emergencies and dangers that recur in every generation.

Liberals and civil libertarians must stand strong against those on the left, as well as the right, who would sacrifice the liberties of their enemies to serve the interests of their friends.

The New McCarthyism Comes to Harvard Law School

A petition recently signed by hundreds of Harvard law school students and alumni raises the specter of the new McCarthyism coming to the law school at which I taught for half a century. The petition states that "Harvard Law School faces a choice of whether to welcome the architects and backers of the Trump administration's worst abuses back into polite society." It demands that Harvard not "hire or affiliate" with any of these sinners, and threatens that "if it does so the school will be complicit if future attacks on our democracy are even more violent – and more successful."

The petition sees this ban as part of the educational and employment mission of the school: "It would also teach ambitious students of all ages that attempting to subvert the democratic process" will deny them access to the "revolving door to success and prestige." This self-serving defense of censorship is intended to convey a crass economic threat: if you want to get a good job after law school, make sure that Harvard bans teachers and speakers who are trying to "rehabilitate their reputations and obscure the stain of their complicity in the Trump administration. . . ."

This is similar to the message that the original McCarthyites tried to have Harvard convey in the 1950s, when students were denied editorship of the Law Review, clerkship recommendations, and other opportunities, which they had earned, because of their alleged affiliation with Communism and other left-wing causes. One would have thought that current Harvard Law School students would be familiar with the sordid history of McCarthyism that infected many American universities, including Brooklyn College, which I attended as an undergraduate and where I fought against the denial of civil liberties to suspected communists.

One would also think that signatories would be aware that if these vague criteria–anti-democratic, racist, xenophobic, and immoral—were applied across the board, they would result in bans on anyone who was associated with the current regimes in China, Cuba, Turkey, Belarus, Russia, Venezuela, the Palestinian Authority, and other repressive governments. It would also apply to supporters of American anti-democratic and anti-free speech groups, such as Antifa, and the very organization—People's Parity Project—that is promoting this anti-free speech petition. Indeed, historically, repression and censorship have been directed primarily against the left. Even today, the French government is expressing concern about the impact of "islamo-leftist" influences from American universities.

The Harvard Law School petition is directed only at Trump supporters, not supporters of left-wing anti-democratic repression, either here or abroad. It is based on the assumption that there is a special "Trump exception" to freedom of speech and due process. But exceptions to free speech and academic freedom for some risk becoming the rule for all.

Free speech for me but for not for thee is not a defensible principle. Today, it is the mantra of the new censors, who demand deplatforming and cancellation of speakers, teachers, and writers who disagree with their anti-Trump zealotry. But the voracious appetite of the censor is rarely sated. Some are now trying to silence defenders of the Constitution, like me, who opposed most of Trump's policies, but who also opposed what we believe were unconstitutional efforts to impeach him. When I was invited to speak by a Harvard Law School student group, the event had to be moved off campus as the result of threats to shout me down and silence me.

Much of this effort to exclude Trump supporters from campuses comes from individuals and organizations that also demand more "diversity." But their definition of diversity is limited to race, gender, sexual orientation, and ethnicity. It doesn't extend to the central mission of universities: to hear and learn from the widest array of views, perspectives, ideologies, and political preferences.

Today's students should welcome Trump supporters and challenge them— respectfully, civilly, and with open minds. They should be willing to listen to views diametrically opposed to their own deeply felt morality and politics. Many of these views, wrong as they may be on their merits and demerits, are accepted by tens of millions of American voters. Those of us who disagree with these views should feel confident that they will be soundly rejected in the open marketplace of ideas, as they were in the 2020 election. But no university or law school should shut down this marketplace, as the old McCarthyism did and this new McCarthyism is now trying to do. There is no place for selective censorship based on political affiliation at the Harvard Law School or any institution of higher education that receives federal or state funding. This anti-civil liberties petition should be rejected in the marketplace of ideas and by all students, faculty, and administrators who value diversity of opinions both inside and outside the classroom.

Two Members of Congress Want to Re-Introduce McCarthyite "Red Channels"

Two Democratic members of congress from the Silicon Valley area have written official letters to cable and satellite carriers urging them to shut down conservative TV channels. These letters are reminiscent of those written by Senator Joseph McCarthy and his henchmen back in the early 1950s, urging Television networks and Hollywood studios to drop suspected Communists or leftists. (Remember the movie *The Front*).

The shoe is now on the other foot—it is the left that is trying to censor the right—but it is causing just as many calluses on our First Amendment. All decent people who care about freedom of speech, without regard to right or left, must stand strongly in opposition to the censorial pressures being exerted by these benighted members of Congress.

Nor are these two alone. Congressional committees are now meeting to discuss ways of dealing with "disinformation and extremism in the media."

As with McCarthyism, this attack on free speech is directed only against one side of the political spectrum. This time it is focusing only on conservative news media. The letter from the members of Congress ends with a veiled threat: "Are you planning to continue carrying Fox News, One American News Network, and Newsmax on your platform, both now and beyond the renewal date? If so, why?"

In their letter, the two members of Congress—Anna G. Eshoo and Jerry McNerney—complain only about "right-wing media outlets." Not a word is said about left-wing media outlets, such as CNN and MSNBC, which deny their viewers facts and information that might influence their decisions in a nuanced manner.

CNN is especially guilty of doctoring videos, editing soundbites, distorting the truth, and presenting one-sided diatribes. But this doesn't concern Eshoo and McNerney, because CNN presents *their* side of the narrative. "Free speech for me but not for thee," seems to be their approach. They would like to see network cable television become the Democratic party's "Pravda." And, like the Soviet Union, they would like to take down all opposing views and deny them access to cable and satellite carriers. They ignore the provision of the Bill of Rights which prohibits Congress from making any law or taking any action that abridges the freedom of speech.

A letter from two members of Congress on official Congressional stationery to satellite and cable carriers carries the imprimatur of government. Holding one-sided hearings that focus only on "right-wing media outlets" constitutes a direct threat to these carriers.

The most dangerous aspect of what these members of Congress are doing is that they surely believe they are acting in the interest of truth, liberalism, and the American Way. Nothing could be further from the truth. Left-wing censors are as dangerous as right-wing censors. Left-wing McCarthyism is as immoral as right-wing McCarthyism. Well-intentioned censorship is even more dangerous than censorship that is overtly motivated by evil intentions.

Newsmax and Fox should challenge any congressional hearings that deal with the contents of their shows. They should refuse to answer questions from Congress regarding their news gathering or presentation. The government has no business being in their news or editorial rooms. The First Amendment protects them from such unconstitutional intrusions.

Not only should Fox and Newsmax fight back against these efforts to control and censor them, so should the satellite and cable providers that carry them.

In the golden era of the First Amendment—from about 1960 to 2000—the ACLU could be counted on to take up this battle. Don't hold your breath. The current ACLU prioritizes partisan politics, and especially hatred of any-thing Trump, over freedom of speech, especially conserva-tive or pro-Trump speech. They have gotten very rich based on this shift in priorities, because too few Americans believe in free speech for thee as well as me. So all Americans who care about our shrinking First Amendment must take up their cudgels and fight for our liberties.

CHAPTER 3

Violent Responses to
Speech and Incitement

It has been said that assassination is the ultimate form of censorship. We have seen violence used—both by governments and private persons—in an effort to stop and or punish speech. I have written articles about this attack on free speech for many years.[31]

---

31   I was interviewed about the terrorist massacre at the offices of *Charlie Hebdo* for an article entitled "Alan Dershowitz: France Reaped What it Sewed in Paris Attack:" While France is reeling from the terrorist massacre of 12 people at the Paris offices of a satirical magazine, the country is also "one of the worst when it comes to rewarding terrorism," lawyer and author Alan Dershowitz told "MidPoint" host Ed Berliner on Newsmax TV.

"They plan with everybody. They reward every terrorist," Dershowitz said of the French. "They've never been part of the International campaign against terrorism. They are part of the problem, not part of the solution." The magazine, which was fire-

A. Beheading in Nice not an Isolated Act, Fits a Disturbing Pattern.

[On October 30th, 2020, I wrote about efforts by radical Islamists to suppress speech in France.]

The murder of three French citizens in a Nice church, one by beheading, was an act of terrorism, apparently by an Islamic extremist shouting, "*Allahu Akbar!*"

It's not an isolated incident.

---

bombed in 2011, has mocked radical Islamists in the past, but has also belittled some critics of Muslim religion and culture as Islamophobias and fear mongers. Dershowitz said that the attack should come as no surprise, given Europe's history of tolerating Islamic terrorism. "We have tolerated extreme Islamic terrorism from the very beginning," he said, describing the Palestinian state as "born in terrorism," with the assent of governments including France and Germany. "When the Israeli athletes were murdered in Munich (in 1972), most European countries freed them when they came to their country," said Dershowitz. "Germany let them go, and most European countries have freed terrorists. It shouldn't surprise anybody in Europe, they've never fought terror."

It is not clear what kind of attack or carnage it will take for Europe to say, in effect, this time is different, and commit fully to fighting violent Islamic extremism, said Dershowitz. We've said that every time there's been a terrorist attack and it just doesn't happen," he said. Dershowitz also said that radical Islam enjoys support from "millions of people" in the Muslim world "who support terrorism, who will be applauding what happened today."

Not tens, hundreds or thousands," he said, "but millions will be supporting what happened today. It's very, very big problem. The reason it has so many supporters is because it works. Terrorism works. It achieves the goals and results. Palestinians would not be getting a state today if it wasn't for their terrorists."

It's part of a pattern of violence that reflects incitement by some Islamic extremist leaders who preach violence as a legitimate response to what they deem insults directed at their prophet.

The insults can be as slight as depicting the prophet in cartoon or other visual form, even if he is not presented in a negative way.

We all recall the mass murder of artists and others who worked at the magazine *Charlie Hebdo,* which had published cartoons of the prophet.

Then there was the beheading of a school teacher who had apparently used some of these cartoons in teaching about freedom of speech.

Now, we have the most recent beheading and stabbings, following on the heels of provocative calls by Turkish dictator Erdogan for "retaliation" against France for insulting Islam.

There is, of course, no evidence that Erdogan's bigoted statements directly caused the recent terrorist attack. But they certainly contributed to an atmosphere in which violence is seen as legitimate retaliation against insults.

It was Dr. Sigmund Freud who once observed that civilization began when the first human hurled an insult instead of a spear. The corollary is that civilization ends when throwing a spear, or wielding a machete, becomes an acceptable response to a hurled or drawn insult.

Nor is Erdogan alone among leaders in the Middle East calling for violent retaliation against perceived slights or insults. The leaders of Hamas, Hezbollah, and even the Palestinian Authority (PA) have called for violent responses to "dirty" Jews praying on the Temple Mount, a place holy both to Judaism and Islam.

Moreover, they pay bounties to Palestinians who kill Jews: pay to slay. They paid the family of a Palestinian who murdered an American soldier visiting Israel. This led to a suspension by Congress of some aid to the Palestinian Authority.

In our own country, there have been calls by some right-to-life extremists to engage in violence to prevent the "genocide of the unborn." Several doctors who provided abortions have been killed and injured.

I have been threatened with violence on several occasions on account of my political views, especially with regard to Israel and Jewish issues. I have needed armed guards while speaking at some universities.

This is what we have come to in today's world, where "free speech for me but for not thee" has become the norm at some universities, in many media, and in some political circles.

To be certain, there is a difference between beheading someone whose speech has offended you and merely censoring them. But as a great philosopher warned, those who begin by burning books end up burning people.

Assassination is the ultimate form of censorship, as we should be reminded by the murder of Yitzhak Rabin, who was killed because he advocated a two-state solution to the Israeli-Palestinian conflict.

Anwar Sadat and King Abdallah suffered the same fate for advocating peace.

So we must oppose all forms of censorship, from the most extreme to the relatively benign, such as selective rejection of content by Twitter, Facebook, and other social media behemoths.

Once we begin to accept the premises underlying the call for censorship, it becomes largely a matter of degree where we start and stop.

B. Fakhrizadeh and Soleimani Were Even More Justified Killings than Bin Laden

[On December 14th, 2020, I wrote about the targeted assassination of an Iranian scientist who was helping Iran secure a nuclear arsenal]

Former CIA Director John Brennan recently condemned the targeted assassination of Iranian nuclear scientist Mohsen Fakhrizadeh, calling it "a criminal act" and a flagrant violation of international law. Senator Bernie

Sanders rushed to join in the condemnation, decrying the killing as "murder."

At the same time, Brennan defended the assassination of Osama bin Laden, which occurred during his tenure and was ordered by his former boss, President Barack Obama. Sanders went even further at the time, "applaud[ing]" the killing of bin Laden and calling it "a historic moment in our fight against terrorism."

Yet, by any standards of law, morality, and common sense, the assassination of Fakhrizadeh, as well as the earlier assassination of Iranian Revolutionary Guard Corps-Quds Force Commander Qassem Soleimani—both done during President Donald Trump's presidential tenure—were far more justified than even the assassination of Osama bin Laden himself.

Both Fakhrizadeh and Soleimani posed ongoing threats to innocent civilians. At the time of his death, Soleimani was actively planning terrorist attacks against the United States and its allies. Fakhrizadeh was working on the development of a nuclear arsenal for Iran, whose leaders threatened (and still threaten) to use it to murder millions of innocent Israelis and other civilians. The targeted assassinations of these two threats to humanity were fundamentally preventative, in nature.

Osama bin Laden, on the other hand, was a has-been fugitive hiding in a remote location with no contact to the outside world, and no realistic threat of future terrorism. His killing was pure revenge for what he had done in the past. It was, to be sure, justifiable revenge for his ordering the murder of thousands of Americans in the 9/11 attacks. He deserved to be brought to justice—to be placed on trial, if possible. However, the order to the Navy SEALs was apparently not to capture him alive, but to kill him and bury his body at sea. Brennan presumably approved those orders, despite the reality that bin Laden at the time posed no discernible future danger.

I have little moral concern about how Osama bin Laden was handled, but it follows *a fortiori* that if his *revenge* killing was justified, then the *preventative* killings of Fakhrizadeh and Soleimani were even more justified.

The fact that Fakhrizadeh and Soleimani worked for Iran—a nation and thus distinguishable from al-Qaeda, a jihadist outfit—should make no legal or moral difference. They, like bin Laden, were illegal combatants, engaged in crimes against humanity. They, like bin Laden, were leaders of a U.S.-designated terrorist group, the Islamic Revolutionary Guard Corps. Their potential victims— including those in Israel and the United States—had the right to stop them from carrying out their planned carnage against civilians. In all cases, it would be better to capture such war criminals alive, but if that is not possible, it is entirely lawful and moral to neutralize them and the threats they pose while limiting the collateral damage to others. Every law-abiding nation in history has done that in extreme cases like those.

The killing of Osama bin Laden was far more questionable, both legally and morally, especially if there was an order not to take him alive. I can understand such an order, from a pragmatic perspective—his capture might well have stimulated hostage-taking—but there is no legal justification for an advance "shoot to kill" order, assuming one did indeed exist. And morally, it is difficult to justify cold-blooded revenge killings, if that is what was indeed ordered.

Again, I am not writing this to condemn the killing of Osama bin Laden, but rather to demonstrate that the killings of Fakhrizadeh and Soleimani were far *more* justified. I am also writing this to expose the double standard of Brennan, Sanders, and others who justify everything done by President Obama while rushing to condemn analogous actions taken by President Trump (and perhaps Israeli Prime Minister Benjamin Netanyahu) that were, in actuality, far more justified.

Targeted killings of terrorists and other massive threats are inherently controversial. The concept should be studied, debated and discussed. I wrote an entire book about it, entitled *Preemption: A Knife that Cuts Both Ways*. In the book, I set out criteria for the deployment of extrajudicial killings (of which targeted assassination is one genre—others include self-defense, defense of others, and war). One conclusion should be clear: The justification for extrajudicial killings should not depend on who the president—or the CIA head—happens to be at a given moment in time. The prevention of terrorism is too important to become yet another object of partisan bickering.

C. A Yellow Light for Red-Flag Laws

[The continuing gun violence that plagues America led to some proposals that endanger civil liberties. I wrote about these dangers.]

President Trump's proposal to "red flag" potential mass shooters is well-intentioned. If we could prevent even one mass killing by identifying and disarming the potential perpetrator beforehand, it would be worthwhile. But do we have the tools to do it, and at what cost to our constitutional rights?

I have studied, taught, and written for half a century about the difficulties of predicting violence. My first scholarly article, in 1970, was titled "The Law of Dangerousness: Some Fictions About Predictions," and a subsequent book was titled *Preemption: A Knife That Cuts Both Ways* (2006). Research shows that any group of people identified as future violent criminals will contain many more who won't be violent (false positives) than who will (true positives).

More true positives mean more false ones. Such groupings also fail to identify many future violent criminals (false negatives).

We don't yet have the predictive tools necessary to raise the number of true positives while at the same time reducing false positives. We may someday develop such tools, but how many false positives are we willing to tolerate until then to decrease the number of false negatives? Put another way: How many law-abiding people are we prepared to deprive of guns to prevent even one mass shooting?

To those who favor strict gun control, the answer might seem obvious. They think it's worth it for 100 or 1,000 nonviolent people to lose their guns to prevent a mass shooting. But those who regard gun possession as a fundamental right under the Second Amendment—as the Supreme Court ruled in *District of Columbia v. Heller* (2008)—frame the issue differently. They ask: Can the government deprive a citizen of a constitutional right based on a prediction?

Red-flag laws risk setting a dangerous precedent. If the government can take your guns based on a prediction today, what will stop it from taking your liberty based on a prediction tomorrow?

It isn't a far-fetched concern. The U.S. detained more than 100,000 Japanese-Americans during World War II based on wildly exaggerated predictions of sabotage. States lock up convicted sexual predators even after they've completed their sentences based on predictions of recidivism. (The best predictor of future violence is past violence, so sexual-predator laws may have fewer false positives.) Criminal defendants—who are entitled to the presumption of innocence—are frequently denied bail based on predictions that they will flee or commit additional crimes.

So the danger of moving from red-flag gun confiscation to red-flag preventive detention is real. We should be careful about denying individual rights based on questionable predictions. Red-flag laws would be worth trying as a remedy for gun violence if they remained limited to temporary gun confiscation pending a timely due-process review. But when government starts taking away some rights in the interest of safety, all rights are at risk.

D. Can the President Send in Federal Troops to Quell Domestic Violence?

[The question of using federal troops to deal with violence growing out of protests regarding racial discrimination was widely debated. I wrote an op-ed setting out the legal issues.]

President Donald Trump's decision to send federal authorities into several local areas raises important questions under our system of federalism, separation of powers, and checks and balances.

Let's begin with the Constitution, as we must. There are several provisions that may be relevant. There is nothing in Article II, which sets out the powers of the president, that is directly on point. The most relevant phrase is that the president "shall take care that the laws be faithfully executed," but that is a very general provision, applicable to federal laws.

Article IV provides that "the United States shall guarantee to every state in this union a Republican form of government, and shall protect each of them against invasion; and on application of the legislature, *or* of the executive (when the legislature cannot be convened) against domestic violence" (emphasis added). This provision does not specifically empower the president, as distinguished from the United States government in general, to take any action. Moreover, if any action is to be taken, it must be done on application of either the state legislature or the governor. In this case, the president sent federal authorities into states that did not apply for such assistance. So Article IV seems inapplicable.

Article I, which sets out the powers of Congress, not the president, authorizes Congress "to provide for calling for the militia to execute the laws of the union, suppress insurrections and repel invasions." The demonstrations around the country are certainly not invasions; nor, in my view, are they insurrections. Moreover, Congress has not explicitly authorized calling out the militia in this case.

It is argued, however, that Congress has empowered, in 40 U.S.C. § 1315, the secretary of the Department of Homeland Security to "protect the buildings, grounds and property that are owned, occupied or secured by the federal government," or any of its agencies. The president may, of course, direct all Cabinet members to ensure that the laws—including this one—are faithfully executed. This would include arresting federal lawbreakers even away from the areas abutting the building themselves. There are other statutes, as well, that grant limited powers, but 40 U.S.C § 1315 is the most relevant.

In sum, therefore, it would seem as if the president does have the power to send in federal authorities to protect federal property, even over the objection of state and local authorities, but that statutory power does not seem to extend beyond the protection of federal property and personnel. The president does not have the power to police cities, in general, without legislative or gubernatorial authorization.

Another important question, regarding separation of powers, arises as well. Assuming that the president is acting beyond his authority, do the courts have the constitutional power under Article III to order the president to cease and desist? A related question is, who would have standing to raise that issue? If a citizen were hurt by a federal official, perhaps that citizen could raise this issue in a lawsuit. But it is uncertain whether anyone other than an injured plaintiff would have standing to ask the court to order the president to withdraw federal authorities. A federal judge in Oregon ruled that the state attorney general lacked such standing, and other cases are pending.

We are facing unprecedented situations, and it should not be surprising that the law does not provide crystal-clear guidance on the powers of the president in emergency circumstances. Back in the early 1970s, I wrote a series of scholarly articles about the law in times of crisis. After researching cases going back to the Founding of our nation, I summarized the precedents as follows:

"Our past experiences suggest the following outline: The courts—especially the Supreme Court—will generally not interfere with the executive's handling of a genuine emergency while it still exists. They will employ every technique of judicial avoidance at their disposal to postpone decisions until the crisis has passed. (Indeed, though thousands of persons have been unlawfully confined during our various periods of declared emergency, I am aware of no case where the Supreme Court has ever actually ordered anyone's release while the emergency was still in existence.) The likely exceptions to this rule of judicial postponement will be cases of clear abuse, where no real emergency can be said to exist,

and cases in which delay would result in irrevocable loss of rights, such as those involving the death penalty. Once the emergency has passed, the courts will generally not approve further punishment; they will order the release of all those sentenced to imprisonment or death in violation of ordinary constitutional safeguards. But they will not entertain damage suits for illegal confinement ordered during the course of the emergency."

It is precisely because the courts will be reluctant to interfere with a president's actions that the president himself must be sure that his orders are necessary and justified. The Constitution placed great trust in the discretion of the chief executive. Whether this chief executive has lived up to that trust will be judged by the voters.

E. Exploiting the Floyd Protests to Demonize Israel

[The protests over the George Floyd killing generated some anti-Israel rhetoric, which I wrote about.]

This "blame it on Israel" or "blame it on the Jews" bigotry is common throughout the world at demonstrations for legitimate causes that are unrelated to the Middle East.

As usual, anti-Israel extremists, especially some on the hard left, are trying to exploit the tragic and inexcusable death of George Floyd to level their typical baseless charges against Israel. Signs and chants at several protests have either tried to blame Israel—falsely, as it turns out—for training the policemen who are responsible for Floyd's

death, or to compare police brutality in America with legitimate efforts by the Israel military to prevent acts of terrorism against civilians.

A cartoon that is being circulated on social media
shows an American policeman with his knee on the neck
of an African American man and an Israeli soldier with
his knee on the neck of a Palestinian man. The policeman and soldier are embracing. The caption above reads:
"Black Lives Matter," though there is no evidence that
the organization has anything to do with this bigoted cartoon. A painting of George Floyd wearing a Palestinian
keffiya is also being circulated, and BDS proponents at
the University of California are accusing Israel of training
racist American policemen. Anti-Israel graffiti—"F...K
Israel," "free Palestine"—has been sprayed on synagogue
walls in Los Angeles during anti-racist demonstrations.

This "blame it on Israel" or "blame it on the Jews" bigotry is common throughout the world at demonstrations
for legitimate causes that are unrelated to the Middle East.
Anti-Israel extremists from the hard left try to promote
the intersectionality propaganda that all the evils of the
world are produced by privileged white democracies, such
as the US and Israel. Islamic extremists—who are hard to
classify as left or right—use any excuse to demonize Israel.
Anti-Semitic extremists from the hard right have always
tried to blame the Jews for all of the world's evils. An old

Polish expression summarized it well: "If there is trouble in the world, the Jews must be behind it." Today that has been expanded by the hard left and Islamic extremists to include the nation-state of the Jewish people among those who cause the world's problems, ranging from capitalism, to destruction of the environment, to police violence.

The organization "Black Lives Matter," which does much good, is not immune from this bigotry. Its own platform blames Israel for police violence against African Americans, and compares such violence to what it falsely calls the "genocide" of the Palestinian people. Many good people who support the organization are unaware of its gratuitous demonization of Israel, and would oppose such distractions from its core mission. George Zeiden, a Palestinian activist, has urged his followers to "leave Palestine out of the current protests lest it take attention away from this watershed moment in Black American history." Not everything is about the Palestinians, despite efforts by intersectionalists to make it so, and not everything is about Israel and Jews, despite the obsessive focus of the hard left and hard right on these tiny elements of the issues facing the world.

Historically, the Jews have always been caught between the black of Fascism and the red of Communism. This was true in the 1920s and 1930s in Europe, and there is a danger that it could now manifest itself during this time of extremism, when bigots on both sides are prepared to scapegoat the Jews and their nation state.

Those of us who are both Jewish and Liberal—who support Israel and oppose unjustified police violence—must be willing to participate in and encourage legitimate protests against police violence, such as that caught on video in the Floyd case. We must stand up and be heard in condemnation of such violations—but we must stand up and be heard against those who would exploit tragedies to foment violence against Jews and the nation-state of the Jewish people.

We should not generalize: the vast majority of protesters are focused on the injustices of police misconduct. But we cannot ignore those—even if they are relatively few in number—who would turn these protests into bigoted attacks against Israel. Bigotry unanswered grows in size and intensity.

Silence is not an option in the face of any injustice. Black lives matter greatly; so do Palestinian lives; so do Jewish and Israeli lives. We must not be afraid of being criticized for condemning bigotry on all sides. As the great sage Hillel put it 2000 years ago, "If I am not for myself, who will be for me? If I am not for others, what am I?" He ended his statement with a call to action: "And if not now, when?"

Now is the time to protest the injustice against George Floyd and other African American men and women who have been unjustly targeted by overzealous—and often racist—police. But now is also the time to speak out against those who would hijack this tragic history to manifest the oldest continuing prejudice known to mankind, namely antisemitism.

F. Can the International Criminal Court Declare Palestine to be State?

The highly politicized International Criminal Court just declared statehood for Palestinians. They did it without any negotiation with Israel, without any compromise, and without any recognized boundaries. They also did it without any legal authority, because the Rome Treaty, which established the International Criminal Court, make no provision for this criminal court to recognize new states. Moreover, neither Israel nor the United States are signatories to that treaty, so the decisions of the International Criminal Court are not binding on them. Nor is this divided decision binding on signatories, since it exceeds the treaty authority of the so-called court.

I say "so-called" court because the International Criminal Court is not a real court in any meaningful sense of that word. Unlike real courts, which have statutes and common law to interpret, the International Criminal Court often just makes it up. As the dissenting judge so aptly pointed out, the Palestine decision is not based on existing law. It is based on pure politics. And the politics of the majority decision is based in turn on applying a double standard to Israel—as the United Nations, the International Court of Justice, and other international bodies have long done.

There are numerous other groups —the Kurds, the Chechens, the Taiwanese, and the Tibetans among them— who claim some degree of independence. Yet neither the International Criminal Court nor other international organizations have ever given them the time of day. But the Palestinians—both in West Bank and Gaza— who have refused to negotiate in good faith, and have used terrorism as their primary claim to recognition, have been rewarded for their violence by this decision.

And Israel, which has offered the Palestinians statehood in exchange for peace on several occasions, has been punished for its willingness to negotiate and its determination to protect its citizens from Palestinian terrorism.

There are so many serious war crimes and other violations of humanitarian laws occurring around the world that the International Criminal Court deliberately ignores. The chief prosecutor sees as one of her roles to focus attention away from third-world countries, where many of these crimes occur, and toward Western democracies. What could be a better target for this perverse form of "prosecutorial affirmative action" than Israel? I say perverse because the real victims of such selective prosecution are the third-world citizens of those counties whose leaders are killing and maiming them.

Israel, on the other hand, has the best record on human rights, the rule of law, and concern for enemy civilians of any nation faced with comparable threats.

According to British Military expert Richard Kemp, "No country in the history of warfare has done more to avoid civilian casualties than Israel did in Operation Cast Lead." Israel's Supreme Court has imposed daunting restrictions on its military and has provided meaningful remedies for criminal acts committed by individual Israeli soldiers. The role of the International Criminal Court, according to the treaty, is to intrude on the sovereignty of nations only if those nations are not capable of administering justice. The principle of "complementarity" is designed to allow courts in democratic nations, like Israel, to address their own problems within the rule of law. Only if the judiciary totally fails to address these problems does the court have jurisdiction, *even* in cases involving signatories to the treaty, which Israel is not.

The United States should reject the International Criminal Court decision not only because it is unfair to its ally Israel, but because it sets a dangerous precedent that could be applied against the United States and other nations that operate under the rule of law. Israel should challenge the decision, but should cooperate in any investigation, because the truth is its best defense. Whether an investigation conducted by the International Criminal Court can produce the truth is questionable, but the evidence—including real-time video and audio—will make it more difficult for ICC investigators to distort reality.

All in all, the International Criminal Court decision on Palestine is a setback for a single standard of human rights. It is a victory for terrorism and an unwillingness to negotiate peace. And it is a strong argument against the United States and Israel joining this biased "court" and giving it any legitimacy.

Looking Backward to Show Us the Way Forward

The First Amendment has been under attack since its birth in 1791. It was nearly still-born. Within just a few years, Congress—which was prohibited from making any law abridging free speech—enacted the Alien and Sedition Acts of 1798, which not only abridged the freedoms of speech and of the press, but virtually abolished them. These repressive laws were supported by large numbers of Americans, including their most popular president, George Washington.

When Thomas Jefferson defeated Adams as president, he essentially rescinded the Alien and Sedition Acts and freed those who were in prison pursuant to these federal laws, but he encouraged states to impose restrictions on seditious speech. Although, in his writings, Jefferson was a free speech purist, in practice, he, too, often supported free speech for him but not for them, for me but not for thee.

Few presidents throughout our history have actively supported First Amendment freedoms, especially for a hostile press. During war times, the First Amendment was often compromised along with other constitutional safe-guards. Secrecy and classification rules interfered with press freedoms. Self-censorship, imposed in the name of patriotism, inhibited honest reporting.

In the early part of the 20th century, liberal presidents such as Woodrow Wilson cracked down on freedom of speech for radicals, especially immigrants from foreign countries. The notorious Palmer Raids were a frontal attack on freedom of expression and association.

In the middle of the 20th century, McCarthyism reared its ugly head. It received the cooperation of many in the media, universities, and business. It, too, was popular among many Americans. We were fortunate that its per-sonification, Senator Joseph McCarthy, was such a buf-foon and so unlikeable. Had he been more charismatic, McCarthyism might have endured beyond the 1950s.

We experienced the golden age of freedom of speech, press, and assembly from the end of McCarthyism to the beginning of the new censorship in the 21st century. During that nearly half a century, a Supreme Court majority built on the dissenting opinions of earlier justices led by Louis Brandeis, Oliver Wendell Holmes, Jr., and Robert Jackson. Chief Justice Warren, along with Justices Black, Douglas, Brennan, Steward, Goldberg, and Fortas led the way. I was privileged to serve as a law clerk both on the Court of Appeals and the Supreme Court during that period, helping to draft important First Amendment decisions. I also participated in the litigation of several of the most important First Amendment cases. These included the *Pentagon Papers* case, the *I Am Curious (Yellow)* case, the *Hair* case, the *Titticut Follies* case, the *Chicago 7* case, the *Deep Throat* case, the *Bruce Franklin* case, the *Wikileaks* case, and many others involving anti-war protests by students and faculty members. As a board member of the ACLU, I was involved in many other cases, including the Neo-Nazi march through Skokie and many civil rights demonstrations. These cases and others, such as *New York Times vs. Sullivan*, *Brandenburg v. Ohio*, and *Falwell v. Hustler* established strong precedents against governmental censorship. The civil rights movement generated support for the right to assemble in protest. This right was applied not only to good protests by Martin Luther King, but equally to bad protests by the Nazi party and the KKK. The First Amendment thrived. It wasn't broken, so few wanted to fix it.

Now we are seeing a regression toward restrictions on freedom of expression. This regression is manifest, at least for now, more in the attitudes of young thought leaders and older anti-Trump zealots than in the opinions of courts. But that will change, since courts reflect public attitudes— sometimes leading them, more often following them.

The Trump presidency accelerated a repressive trend that had begun years earlier. President Trump's speeches and actions provoked a reaction against untrammeled freedom of speech. Academics and pundits twisted the Constitution to fit their desires to exclude Trump and his followers from its protections.

The social media, unconstrained by the First Amendment, imposed their own brand of private censorship and restrictions. Universities, both private and public, adopted speech codes that restricted freedom of expression. "Cancel culture" imposed heavy costs on those who persisted in expressing politically incorrect views. Economic boycotts also targeted those who expressed such views.

The golden age of freedom of speech is gone. It has been tarnished by attitudes that prioritize other good and important values. The irony is that during the golden age of freedom of speech, these other values flourished as well. It was also the genesis of a relatively golden age for equality, for sensitivity to issues of race, gender, and ethnicity, for the environment. We were a better society when freedom of speech was widely respected. We were less divided, less intolerant, less angry with each other. We are moving in the wrong direction. It is unclear whether the attitudinal change away from freedom of speech is a cause or effect of our societal disintegration, but it is surely related. I am convinced we are a better society with more freedom of speech than with less— that those who prioritize other good values over the values of the First Amendment will hurt both. It is a lose-lose game, while strengthening the First Amendment and using it to advocate for other good values is a win-win game— at least in the long run. But we live in a short-run world, in which many decent people are willing to weaken our freedom of speech in an effort to win short-term advantages for other priorities.

Look where that has taken us. It's not a pretty picture. And it's getting worse. So am I an optimist or pessimist? In Israel, they say a pessimist is someone who says, "*Oy vey*, things are so bad, they can't get any worse." The optimist replies, "Yes they can!" I think things can and will get worse if we weaken our freedom of speech. But they can and will get better if we return to the golden age of both freedom and equality.

What then can we realistically expect for the future of free speech in America? The Talmud observed that prophecy ended with the destruction of the Holy Temple. And that anyone who seeks to predict the future is either a fool or a knave. Or perhaps a retired law professor, who has struggled to protect freedom of speech for more than 65 years. So here are my predictions, based on experience, study, and perhaps a bit of wishful thinking:

- The attack on freedom of speech will abate somewhat now that Trump is out of office and his second impeachment is over. Those who were willing to constrain, narrow, shrink, distort, or even abolish the First Amendment in the interest of preventing the dangers they saw coming from the Trump presidency may now come to recognize that the short-term benefits of "getting" Trump are not worth the long-term sacrifices to the First Amendment. It is unlikely that many of them will publicly acknowledge that they made these tradeoffs. Instead, they will find ways not to generalize the compromises they were willing to accept for Trump. They will simply choose the way of the hypocrite: Apply a double standard without admitting their inconsistency. Lawyers and intellectuals are experts at manipulating the facts, the law, and other aspects of reality to cover their double standards. As the French writer François de la Rochefoucauld put it: "hypocrisy is the homage vice pays to virtue."

  To which I would add: Perhaps it is better to apply a hypocritical double standard to freedom of speech than to keep applying the same very bad standard that has recently been selectively applied to Trump and his supporters, enablers, lawyers and associates.

- Although the movement to constrain freedom of speech will abate somewhat, the widespread skeptical attitudes toward this freedom, especially among young progressives, will persist. We will not see, in the short- or middle-term, a return to the attitudes that generated the "golden age" of freedom of speech. Perhaps in the longer-term, when we have experienced the negative consequences of our diminishing respect for the First Amendment, attitudes will change. As I wrote in my book *Rights from Wrongs*:

Rights *come from human experience*, particularly experience with injustice. We learn from the mistakes of history that a rights-based system and certain fundamental rights—such as freedom of expression, freedom of and from religion, equal protection of the laws, due process, and participatory democracy—are essential to avoid repetition of the grievous injustices of the past. Working from the bottom up, from a dystopian view of our experiences with injustice, rather than from the top down, from a utopian theory of perfect justice, we

> build rights on a foundation of trial, error, and our
> uniquely human ability to learn from our mistakes
> in order to avoid replicating them.

One can only hope that the coming generation will learn from the mistakes of their predecessors, especially the mistakes involving compromises with freedom of speech to achieve short-term political benefits.

- The courts will move slowly in cutting back on First Amendment rights, because most judges are neither young nor radical. But, over time, courts come to reflect emerging changes in attitudes. There were only a few free speech cases decided during the Trump administration, but there are several important ones on the horizon, especially defamation cases against Trump lawyers and media supporters. It takes time for litigation to work its way through the court system, so these cases are not likely to be definitively resolved for several years. It is difficult to predict, therefore, what impact the Trump effect—provocative speech followed by efforts to punish or constrain it—may have on these decisions. But the trend away from maximum protection of speech seems likely to impact the courts, as well as other institutions of government.

- The social media will waffle. They will try various approaches to legitimating some form and degree of censorship or cautionary warnings. None will be completely satisfactory. Facebook's attempt to create a "Supreme Court of Censorship" will fail. Its first "decisions" have revealed the problems more than the solutions. The decisions they have made—restoring anti-Muslim and anti-Azerbaijani posts; a quote by Nazi leader Joseph Goebbels; a post that characterized Hydroxychloroquine as "harmless"; and an image of breasts in a post about cancer awareness —seem relatively easy.

  How they deal with Trump and his associates may be more telling. But in the end, it is clear that some censorship must exist: child pornography; classified secrets; descriptions of how to make illegal and dangerous weapons. The hard questions relate to dangerous quack medical treatments; dangerous lies and defamations; overt racial or other bigoted content. These will all be matters of opinion and degree about which reasonable people can disagree.

- There will be changes in Section 230 that currently gives social media total immunity from defamation suits for material posted on its platforms. As social media becomes more like traditional publishers—picking and choosing what to allow— the Congress and the courts will treat them more like traditional publishers, which can be sued if they chose to publish defamatory material. In general, we will see more legislative and judicial attention being paid to social media and increasing efforts to hold them accountable. In addition, there will be more antitrust and related suits seeking to break up the giant monopolies that currently have so much control over the flow of information.

The law is currently playing catch up with technology. The Framers of the First Amendment could not imagine that Americans would be receiving their information in the manner they now receive it. Even more recent laws, such as Section 230, were not based on current realities. We will see new legislation, new congressional hearings, and new judicial decisions governing the internet. Nor will these efforts be limited to the United States. Social media are transnational and recognize no boundaries, despite efforts by some counties to control the flow of information to their citizens. International treaties will be signed in an effort to limit the current confusion growing out of conflicting laws and enforcement priorities. In the end, technology will advance more quickly than the law. And the law will continue to play catch-up.

- In the end, freedom of speech will endure, perhaps a bit wounded, perhaps made stronger by adversity. It will be up to us—the citizens of this great nation—whether liberty lives or dies in the hearts of our men and women.